ROAD TO CORONATION

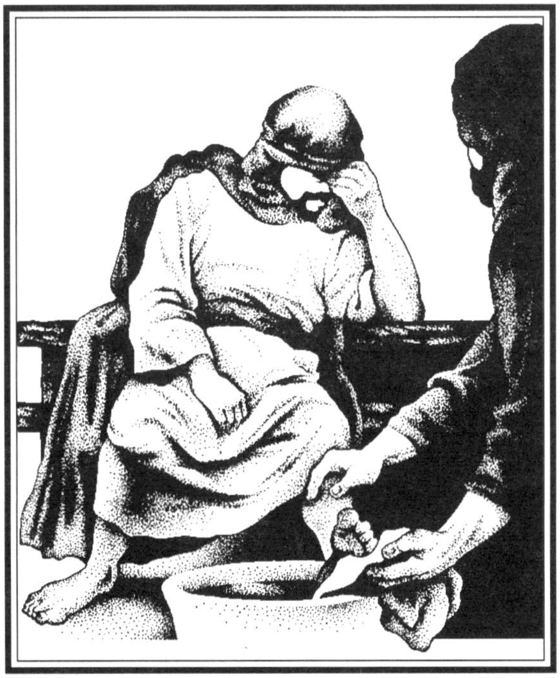

Harry Wendt

Crossways International
Minneapolis, MN

ROAD TO CORONATION

was developed and written by
Harry Wendt, Minneapolis, MN

Illustrations by Knarelle Beard, Adelaide, South Australia

ROAD TO CORONATION

is published and distributed by
CROSSWAYS INTERNATIONAL
7930 Computer Avenue South
Minneapolis, MN 55435
U.S.A.

www.crossways.org

⚜ FORE WORD ⚜

THE JOURNEY FROM DREAM TO TRUTH

What constituted the messianic hope of religious Jews in Jesus' day? What hopes do some religious Jews continue to embrace today? A comment by L.C. Freudmann provides an answer (*Anti-Semitism in the New Testament:* Lanham, University Press of America, 1994, p. 37):

> [Jesus] neither established universal peace, nor did he redeem Israel....For [the Messiah's] coming, according to prophetic promises, will usher in the redemption of Israel from exile... and herald Zion as the acknowledged religious, moral and political center of all nations.

According to Freudmann, when the Messiah finally comes, the eyes of all nations will focus on Jerusalem, which will play *the central role in all aspects of the continuing history of the world.* This dream prevailed also in Jesus' day.

In Matthew, Mark and John, though Jesus goes to Jerusalem, He begins and ends His ministry in Galilee – and spends most of His time there. He goes to Jerusalem only for the events of Holy Week and His crucifixion (referred to in this study as His *coronation*), but after His resurrection He returns to Galilee, Matthew 28, Mark 16:7, John 21.

In Malachi 3:1 we read, "See, I am sending my messenger to prepare the way before me, and the Lord whom you seek *will suddenly come to his temple*." These words are picked up in Mark 1:1 where we read, "See, I am sending my messenger ahead of you, who will prepare your way."

In the Gospels, John the Baptist is the messenger who prepares the way before the divine Jesus, and Jesus is the Lord *who eventually comes to His Temple*. When Jesus comes to His Temple, what does He see, and what does He do, and what results from His actions? The answers play a pivotal role in determining the nature of Jesus' Messiahship, and the Kingdom He came to establish.

In Mark's Gospel, Jesus enters the Temple on a Sunday, looks around at what is going on within it, and then goes back to Bethany. He returns the next day, Monday, and attacks the sacrificial and sales "system" within the Temple, 11:1-19.

Robert Hamerton-Kelly presents us with a vivid description of the Temple system *as it was in Jesus' day* when he writes (*The Gospel and the Sacred*: Minneapolis, Fortress Press, pp. 15,16):

> The Temple stood as a sign for the need of victims; every day it offered public and private sacrifices for the good of society. It was the supreme religious and political institution in Judea at the time of Jesus.
>
> It overshadowed Jerusalem and dominated life in the city. Eighty percent of employment in Jerusalem depended on the Temple, not only on its day to day ritual needs but also on the periodic pilgrim festivals and the ongoing building project which it constituted. Nine thousand priests and Levites worked there, although not at the same time, operating what was in fact a giant abbatoir. The twice-daily official sacrifices on the vast ever-burning altar consumed thousands of animals and forests of wood. There were cattle pens on the north side and sometimes the water of the Kidron stream where the blood was flushed became so thick that it was sold to farmers as fertilizer. Over it all hung a pall of smoke from burning flesh, and when the great pilgrim festivals, like Passover, were in full swing, the priests

> stood in blood sacrificing the victims of private offerings. Jews were expected to make the pilgrimage to the Temple three times a year – twice in the spring – at Passover and Pentecost–and once in the fall, at Succoth. Therefore Jerusalem thrived on what today would be called the convention business. This combination of smoke, blood, and business, whose priests were in league with Roman power to preserve their office and their landed interests, was the historical reality of the sacred for the Gospel of Mark.

Four days after Jesus attacks this system, His coronation takes place. Ironically, the decision finally to do away with Jesus is made by the Sanhedrin whose traditional meeting place was the Royal Porch of the Temple.

As we have already noted, beyond His coronation and resurrection, Jesus and the disciples return to Galilee. At this point in the narrative, how well do the disciples understand what Jesus had been teaching them? According to Acts 1:12, Jesus' ascension took place from the Mount of Olives, just east of the Temple. Just prior to the ascension, the disciples ask Jesus, "Lord, is this the time when You will restore the kingdom to Israel?", Acts 1:6. Their question reflects the hopes expressed in Freudmann's comments above. No doubt it took the ascension event to force them to rethink all that Jesus has been teaching them in relation to life in His kingdom. And, no doubt, during the days between Jesus' ascension and Pentecost, the disciples conduct the most intense small-group Bible study ever held. They have to grapple with questions such as, "What was Jesus really saying to us? What is He asking of us?"

One of the most remarkable descriptions of the challenge Jesus posed to the people of His day, and continues to pose to humanity, is that penned by H.G. Wells (*The Outline of History*, Vol. 1, pp. 425,6):

> Jesus was too great for His disciples. And in view of what He plainly said, is it any wonder that all who were rich and prosperous felt a horror of strange things, a swimming of their world at His teaching? Perhaps the priests and rulers and rich men understood Him better than His followers. He was dragging out all the little private reservations they had made from social service into the light of a universal religious light. He was like a terrible moral huntsman, digging mankind out of the snug burrows in which they had lived hitherto. In the white blaze of His kingdom there was to be no property, no privilege, no pride and no precedence, no motive and reward but love. Is it any wonder that men were dazzled and blinded, and cried out against Him? Even His disciples cried out when He would not spare them that light. Is it any wonder that the priests realized that between this Man and themselves there was no choice, but that He or their priestcraft should perish? Is it any wonder that the Roman soldiers, confronted and amazed by something soaring over their comprehension and threatening all their disciplines, should take refuge in wild laughter, and crown Him with thorns and robe Him in purple and make a mock Caesar of Him? For to take Him seriously was to enter into a strange and alarming life, to abandon habits, to control instincts and impulses, to essay an incredible happiness. Is it any wonder that to this day this Galilean is too much for our small hearts?

Leslie D. Weatherhead writes in *Over His Own Signature*:

> If Christ is, as I believe, the Son of God, the clearest and highest revelation of God's nature and purpose, then He is supremely relevant to all of us today and to all phases of our life together. To pretend He does not exist is only to postpone an inevitable encounter, for He waits at the end of every road [we] can take. To move away from Him is chaos and disaster, whether we speak individually, industrially, socially, politically or internationally. To move toward Him is to follow the path of personal integration and world peace.

The above comments, and those which follow in this Lenten study, remind us that those who claim Jesus as Savior and Lord are called to be life-long students of Jesus' message, and life-long apprentices in His mission.

⚜ Introduction ⚜

The first verse of the New Testament, Matthew 1:1, states (NRSV): "An account of the genealogy of Jesus the Messiah, the son of David, the son of Abraham."

When people begin reading the New Testament, the first thing they encounter is a family tree. Studying other people's family trees can be about as interesting as watching paint dry. But let's dig a little deeper.

In his insightful book, *Following Jesus: Biblical Reflections on Discipleship* (Eerdmans, 1995: pp. 24,25), N.T. Wright writes:

> Do you know what the first page of Matthew's Gospel reminds me of? You may know Handel's great Coronation Anthem, *Zadok the Priest.* Think of how it starts. You have a sequence of broken chords, harmless enough, a few little variations. At one point, we think it's going to grow and swell into something important, but it turns away and goes on with its broken chords, this way and that. . . But then, little by little, we sense that it is really going somewhere; it grows and grows again . . .and, when the swell and the surge are about to become unbearable, the whole thing explodes as the choir crashes in:
>
> Zadok the Priest — and Nathan the Prophet—
> ANOINTED SOLOMON KING . . .

Wright goes on to explain how Matthew leads us on a similar journey. We see names like Abraham and David that seem to lead us somewhere, then unfamiliar names that don't seem to lead us anywhere, until we read "Jesus, who is called Messiah, King of the Jews." Let's follow where Matthew leads.

- In the first 18 verses of his Gospel, he confronts us with a list of 42 names, divided into three blocks of 14 names each. It includes some women, not so-called heroines such as Sarah, Rebekah and Rachel, but less glamorous names like Tamar (Genesis 38), Rahab (Joshua 2), Ruth and Bathsheba – women whose praises some of Matthew's contemporaries might have been slow to sing.

- Some of the names in the opening section (1:1–6) are familiar to some readers, at least: Abraham, Isaac, Jacob. Some of the next ones are not. But then come Boaz, Obed, Jesse and David.

- David! There is the *clue – Jesus is descended from David!* Let's trace this clue. When the author of 2 Samuel 7 wrote his account of God promising David a dynasty, he stated five times that David's dynasty would last "forever" (vv. 13, 16, 29). But it did not! It came to an end some time after 560 B.C. during Judah's exile in Babylon.

- The postexilic community continued to hope and dream: One day God will give us back our kings! The opening verse of the New Testament tells us, *A descendant of David has come! He is not a Gentile upstart, but a descendant of Abraham! You have your kings back!*

- Some questions explode from all the Gospel narratives: What kind of a King was Jesus? What kind of a Kingdom did he establish? What does involvement in His Kingdom imply for His followers?

The opening verses of Matthew's Gospel, unmemorable as they first appear, explode with significance in the closing chapters of his Gospel where Jesus' coronation (His crucifixion) is described in some detail. A similar thread runs through all four Gospels: Ultimately each evangelist presents the cross as Jesus' throne. If we are even to begin to understand the majesty and mystery of the cross, we must walk beside Jesus and the disciples on the road that led to the cross. Let the walk begin!

Harry Wendt

CONTENTS

Unit 1

⚜ The Royal Background ⚜

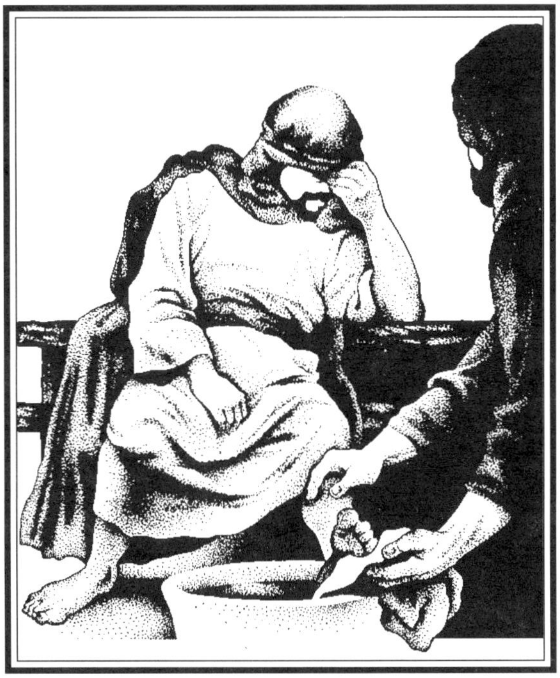

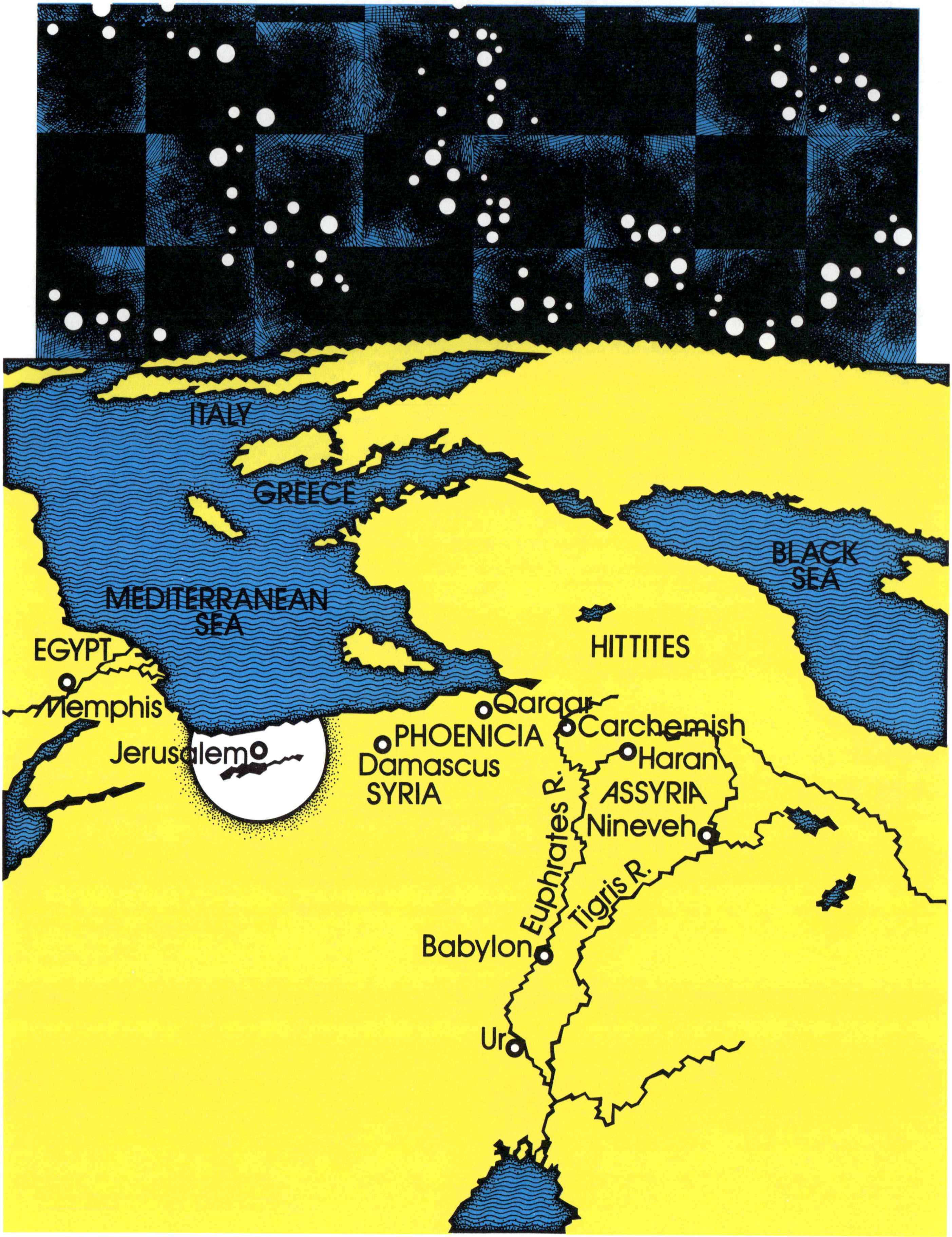
ITALY
GREECE
BLACK SEA
MEDITERRANEAN SEA
EGYPT
HITTITES
Memphis
Qarqar
Carchemish
PHOENICIA
Jerusalem
Damascus
SYRIA
Haran
ASSYRIA
Euphrates R.
Nineveh
Tigris R.
Babylon
Ur

1A

⚜ The Royal Stage ⚜

1. Though the events described in the biblical narrative took place in a small corner of the world, they continue to have worldwide, cosmic and eternal significance.

2. The so-called "Holy Land" (to be referred to as "Israel" in this study) occupied a strategic location politically throughout the Old Testament period. It constituted the land bridge between Egypt to the south, Mesopotamia ("between the rivers," Tigris and Euphrates) to the northeast, and southern Europe to the northwest.

3. The Mesopotamian and southern European nations all aspired to control Egypt. It was, after all, the breadbasket of that corner of the world. The Assyrian armies naturally had to march through Israel to reach Egypt. So did the Babylonian armies. The latter could not take a shortcut to Egypt – it would have taken them across waterless desert. Though travel across deserts became possible with the taming of the camel toward the close of the second millennium B.C., foreign potentates could not place their entire armies on camels. Hence, the way to Egypt was via Israel.

4. Not only did these nations march through Israel; they usually annexed it into their own territories and made it a vassal nation. And because these nations believed their "gods" led their armies into battle, conquering kings traditionally placed images of their gods into the temples of conquered peoples. Naturally, this practice caused problems in Jerusalem!

5. After the reigns of David and Solomon, the Israelites were harassed, conquered, controlled and plundered by neighboring nations. For example, five years after Solomon's death, the Egyptians devastated Judah, plundered Jerusalem, and took Solomon's "treasures" back to Egypt, 1 Kings 14:25,26. (See also section 1D.)

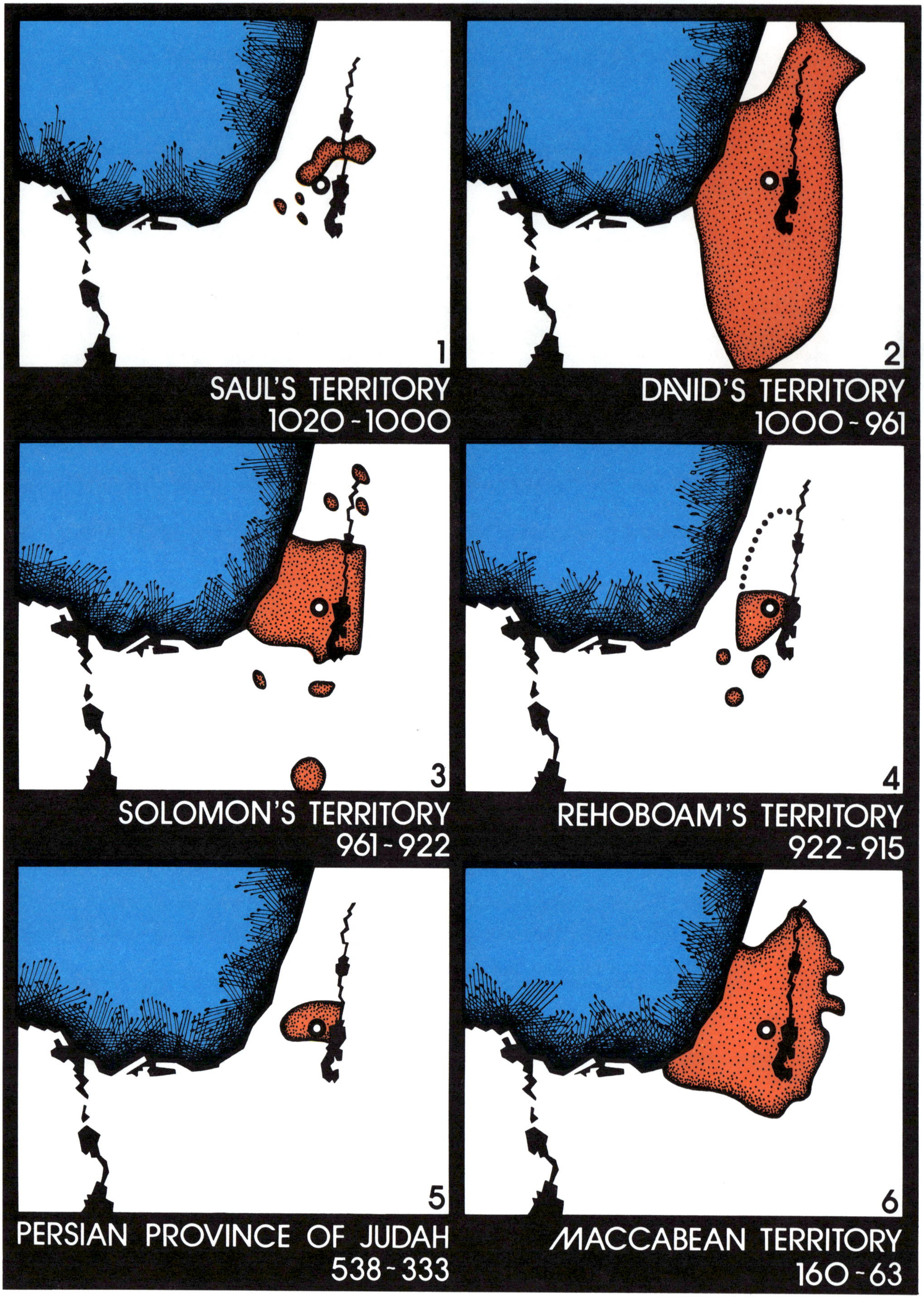
1
SAUL'S TERRITORY
1020 - 1000
2
DAVID'S TERRITORY
1000 - 961
3
SOLOMON'S TERRITORY
961 - 922
4
REHOBOAM'S TERRITORY
922 - 915
5
PERSIAN PROVINCE OF JUDAH
538 - 333
6
MACCABEAN TERRITORY
160 - 63

1B

⚜ The Royal Hope ⚜

Today's European powers might occasionally look back with nostalgia on their former empires. Without doubt, many Jews living in Judea (then a Roman province) at the time of Jesus' birth remembered the realm that once had been theirs! The golden age was during the reign of King David, successor to King Saul; compare frame 2 with frame 5 in illus. 1B.

1. How much territory King Saul controlled is open to question. It is possible that he established the realm David eventually ruled, 1 Samuel 14:47,48. Because King David is the "hero" of the writer of 1 and 2 Samuel and 1 and 2 Kings, the tendency is to downplay Saul and exalt David.

2. David expanded Saul's realm considerably – by brutalizing neighboring peoples and incorporating their territories into his own. Though he subdued the Philistines once and for all, he did not make their land part of his own, 2 Samuel 8:1. He dealt decisively with the Moabites (2 Samuel 8:2), killing two-thirds of their soldiers. He killed 22,000 Syrians and hamstrung many of their chariot horses, 2 Samuel 8:3–8. He slew 18,000 Edomites in the Valley of Salt, 2 Samuel 8:13,14. In dealing with the Arameans and Ammonites, he killed 700 chariot teams and 40,000 horsemen, 2 Samuel 10:18. Though it is possible that these figures are somewhat exaggerated, it is obvious that David's neighbors did not rush to him begging to be incorporated into his realm!

3. Solomon took over his father's realm and possibly initially expanded it, but eventually his kingdom began to crumble. The Edomites broke away (1 Kings 11:14–22); so did the Syrians, 1 Kings 11:23–25. The reason the writer gives for these events is that Solomon did not, like David, worship *one* God in *one* place, *Jerusalem,* 1 Kings 11:4,6. For the writer, this is always the litmus test for the worth of a king. Instead, Solomon worshiped the many gods his foreign wives introduced into his realm, Kings 11:1–13.

4. After Solomon's death, the northern part of his realm broke away, establishing itself as an independent kingdom under Jeroboam, 1 Kings 12:20. The Northern Kingdom was now called Israel, and the Southern Kingdom was called Judah. The two never became one again. Israel was taken into exile in Assyria in 721 B.C. – an event which marked the end of Israel's history.

5. Judah was taken into exile in Babylon in 597 and 587 B.C. The Persians overthrew Babylon in 539 B.C.; the Persian province of Judah was small.

6. Judah's history continued for hundreds of years, though as a vassal to a succession of Near Eastern conquerors; see 1D, p.8. It regained independence during the period of the Hasmoneans, the descendants of the Maccabees, but came under Roman control in 63 B.C.

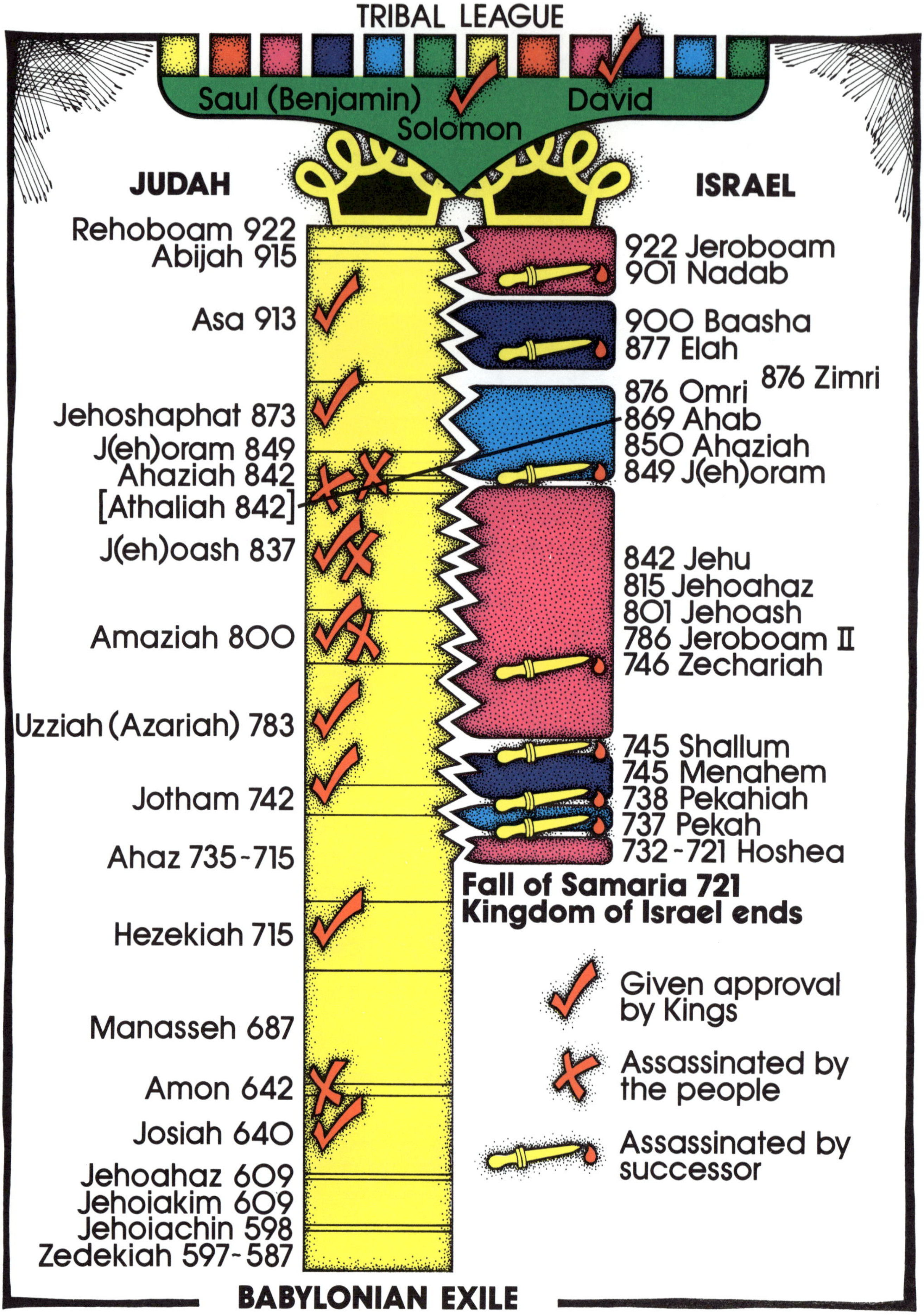
TRIBAL LEAGUE
Saul (Benjamin)
David
Solomon
JUDAH
ISRAEL
Rehoboam 922
Abijah 915
Asa 913
Jehoshaphat 873
J(eh)oram 849
Ahaziah 842
[Athaliah 842]
J(eh)oash 837
Amaziah 800
Uzziah (Azariah) 783
Jotham 742
Ahaz 735-715
Hezekiah 715
Manasseh 687
Amon 642
Josiah 640
Jehoahaz 609
Jehoiakim 609
Jehoiachin 598
Zedekiah 597-587
922 Jeroboam
901 Nadab
900 Baasha
877 Elah
876 Zimri
876 Omri
869 Ahab
850 Ahaziah
849 J(eh)oram
842 Jehu
815 Jehoahaz
801 Jehoash
786 Jeroboam II
746 Zechariah
745 Shallum
745 Menahem
738 Pekahiah
737 Pekah
732-721 Hoshea
Fall of Samaria 721
Kingdom of Israel ends
Given approval by Kings
Assassinated by the people
Assassinated by successor
BABYLONIAN EXILE

1C

⚜ THE ROYAL GENEALOGY ⚜

Who were the kings of Israel prior to the Babylonian devastation in 587 B.C.? 1 and 2 Kings tell us about them, but it's easy to feel at sea trying to make sense of it all! Who was who, and who ruled what? A "Jehoram" ruled the Northern Kingdom of Israel, and a "Jehoram" ruled the Southern Kingdom of Judah. An "Ahaziah" ruled Israel and an "Ahaziah" ruled Judah. A "Jehoash" ruled Israel and a "Jehoash" ruled Judah. Numerous names begin with "Je-" and "Jehoi-." Many of the stories are brutal. Every northern ruler is compared with Jeroboam I and dismissed as evil, e.g. 1 Kings 15:33,34. Some southern kings are praised. How does one make sense out of all this, and what does it all have to do with Jesus? Illus. 1C provides some answers.

1. Three kings held office before the division of the United Kingdom into Israel (north) and Judah (south): Saul, David and Solomon. The kingdom split following Solomon's death.

2. Nine dynasties (a total of 19 kings) then ruled Israel, the Northern Kingdom. Four dynasties consisted of only one person. In seven cases, claimants to the throne assassinated the incumbent; note the seven daggers. Zimri killed himself after only seven days in office.

3. Though a total of 19 kings and one queen ruled Judah, all were descendants of David, with the exception of Queen Athaliah (a daughter of Ahab and Jezebel who married Jehoram of Judah; see 2 Kings 11). There were five assassinations in Judah: Jehu (who became king of Israel) killed Ahaziah, and the latter four assassinations were carried out by "the people of the land" who invariably placed a legitimate descendant of David on the throne.

4. Though every northern king is dismissed as evil (they did not worship in Jerusalem!), ten southern rulers are praised – sometimes with provisos and eventual regrets (e.g. Solomon). They are praised because, like David, they worshiped *one God* (the true God of Israel) in *one place*, the *Jerusalem Temple*. In some cases, they sought also to repair the Temple, support the work of the priests controlling the Temple, and remove foreign and pagan worship practices from the Temple; see 2 Kings 22:1–23:25 and note what Josiah removed from the Temple.

5. Both Jehoiachin (aged 18 in 597 B.C.) and his uncle, Zedekiah (aged 31 in 587 B.C.), were taken into exile in Babylon. Though Zedekiah is never referred to again, 2 Kings 25:27–30 states something of crucial importance:

> In the thirty-seventh year of the exile of King Jehoiachin of Judah [i.e. 560 B.C.], in the twelfth month, on the twenty-seventh day of the month, King Evil-Merodach [*Amel-Marduk, a son of Nebuchadnezzar*] of Babylon, in the year that he began to reign, released King Jehoiachin of Judah from prison; he spoke kindly to him, and gave him a seat above the other seats of the kings who were with him in Babylon. So Jehoiachin put aside his prison clothes. Every day of his life he dined regularly in the king's presence. For his allowance, a regular allowance was given him by the king, a portion every day, as long as he lived.

A descendant of David was still alive in 560 B.C. Though many hoped that King Jehoiachin would survive the exile, return to Jerusalem and reestablish David's line, he died in Babylon. During following centuries, the people longed to get their kings back. Matthew 1:1 says, *You've got them back!*

1D

Royal Dreams

Postexilic Judah was but a shadow of what David's kingdom had been. And to rub salt into the wound, it remained firmly under the control of foreign powers.

1. In 539 B.C., Cyrus of Persia overthrew Babylon, incorporating Babylon's territory into his vast empire. The Jewish exiles living in Babylon looked on Cyrus the Persian (a Gentile!) as God's messiah; see Isaiah 44:24–45:1, especially 44:28, 45:1. After all, Cyrus permitted the Jewish exiles in Babylon to return to Judah and Jerusalem, and even gave them money to fund the rebuilding of the Jerusalem Temple (which Nebuchadnezzar of Babylon had destroyed in 587 B.C.).

2. Though the Jewish exiles were able to return to Judah and eventually rebuild the Temple, Jerusalem and their land, they had no political independence and remained under firm Persian control.

3. After the Persians came the Greeks – under Alexander the Great. The Greeks imposed their way of life and gods on all subject peoples. This culture was called "Hellenism." The vast majority of those living in Greek territories embraced Hellenism gladly, including some in the Holy Land. However, those who adhered to the beliefs and practices of Judaism violently opposed the inroads of Hellenism.

4. After Alexander the Great's death in 323 B.C., his generals struggled to succeed him. In 301B.C., Judah came under the control of the Greek Ptolemies who ruled Egypt. In 198 B.C., Judah came under the control of the Greek Seleucids who ruled Syria.

5. In 165 B.C. the Jewish Maccabees revolted against Syria and gained increasing freedom from the Seleucids. Even so, it was not until 142 B.C. that Judah finally became totally independent.

6. The Maccabees and their descendants, the Hasmoneans, set about building a realm that reflected some of the political glory of David's day. They were often brutal, and at times showed little mercy to their own people. For example, when the hated Alexander Jannaeus (103–76 B.C.) lost a battle against the Nabateans in the Transjordan and many Jews rejoiced over the fact, he had 800 Pharisees crucified in front of his palace balcony as dinner entertainment for him and his concubines.

7. In 63 B.C., Pompey of Rome overran the Jewish territories and incorporated them into the Roman Empire. With the coming of the Romans, dreams died, hopes were born and plots were made! The Romans crushed swiftly and brutally any opposition, especially in Judah, for it lay on that important land bridge between their northern and North African territories. Ongoing hatred of the Romans led to many uprisings against them. *Into such a world came Jesus!*

Unit One

Questions for Reflection

1. Many people think that the Bible focuses on great moral heroes who lived in a rather isolated "Holy Land," and whom we should try to copy. What light does the illustration attached to 1A throw on the validity of this view?

2. Some people believe that God has given us the land in which we live, that we are singularly blessed, and that we should enjoy it. If people in other lands face problems, they should find their own solutions. How would you respond?

3. According to the materials set out in 1C:

   a) Why is every northern king dismissed as evil?

   b) Why are some southern kings described as good?

4. 2 Kings 25:27–30 would have filled many of the exiles living in Babylon with hope. Why?

5. If we lost our political freedom early in the next century, and lived for about 1,000 years under the heel of a series of foreign powers, what cries would go up within the nation, and what actions would result?

How do your answers help you understand attitudes encountered in the biblical narrative?

6. The Romans crushed, brutally and quickly, any political opposition from a vassal nation. In A.D. 6., for example, they killed thousands of zealots, 2,000 by crucifixion. One of the key centers of zealot opposition was Sepphoris, four miles north of Nazareth, Jesus' hometown. Why would Jesus consider these factors when revealing His identity as Messiah?

7. If this country lost possession and control of ninety percent of its present territory, what dreams and movements would become commonplace?

8. Read Psalm 89. What memories and dreams does it express?

Unit 2

⚜ Royal Beginnings ⚜

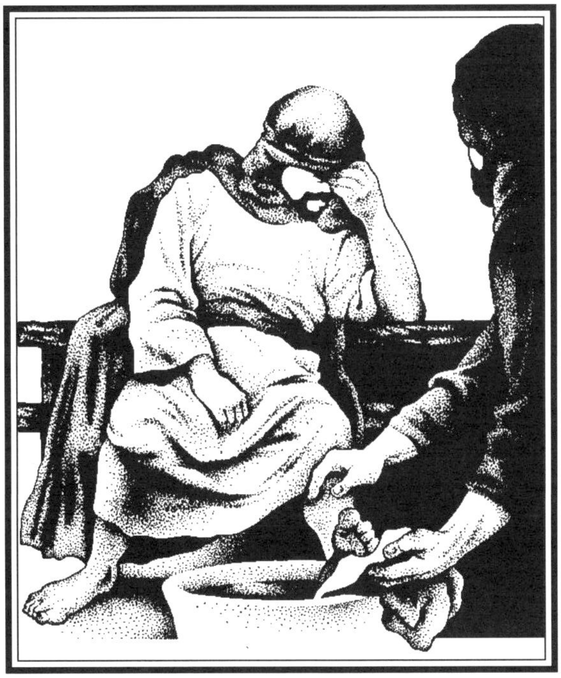

2A

⚜ A Royal City and a Royal Birth ⚜

We now have an overview of the political history of Old Testament times. The personage of King David and the city of Jerusalem loomed very large in that history, and still do today.

1. The day came when King David needed a new capital city. Hebron had served well while he was king of only Judah; Hebron lay, after all, in the center of Judah. But after David gained control also of the northern part of Saul's realm (see 2 Samuel 3:1–5:5), he looked for a city that had previously belonged to neither realm – one that he could call his own. Second Samuel 5:6–10 describes how David captured his new capital, Jerusalem, by wresting it from the Jebusites.

   Capturing Jerusalem was not an easy task. Large walls surrounded it. To complicate matters, the Jebusites mocked him from the top of its walls; they cried out that even the blind and lame could keep David out. But David got into the city and captured it! Apparently his nephew and general, Joab, and a few helpers gained access to the city through a water shaft (which is still there) and made it possible for David's army to enter. In response to the taunt, David had his men kill all the blind and lame in the city, and from that day forth no blind or lame person was permitted to enter the Temple (after it was built by Solomon), 2 Samuel 5:8.

2. Jesus manifested a very different kind of Kingship. Though David wept when forced to leave Jerusalem (2 Samuel 15:30), Jesus wept when He entered it, Luke 19:41. David had killed the blind and the lame when he first entered Jerusalem, but when Jesus entered the city for the first time during His ministry, He healed them, Matthew 21:14. According to Matthew, Mark and Luke, Jesus' ministry took place, by and large, in and around Galilee, and He entered Jerusalem for the first time *during His ministry* five days before His death!

3. David named Jerusalem, "the city of David" (2 Samuel 5:9). However, Jerusalem is never called the city of David in the New Testament. Bethlehem, David's birthplace (1 Samuel 16:1) and Jesus' birthplace, is now called that, Luke 2:4. (At the time of Jesus' birth, Bethlehem's population might have been about 150.) In the Gospels, Jerusalem is viewed as the *city of opposition to Jesus*!

4. David's wife, Bathsheba, had played a powerful role in the affairs of the Israelite kingdom, ensuring that *her* son Solomon succeeded David, 1 Kings 1:11–31. Solomon supplied her with a throne at his right hand, 1 Kings 2:19. The king's mother wielded power!

5. Compare Bathsheba to Mary, the mother of David's descendant, Jesus. Mary was probably only thirteen or fourteen years old when she gave birth to the Christ-child. She had good reason to ponder the origin and significance of the child she would bear, Luke 2:19, 51; see also Luke 1:26–38. Little did she realize that there would come a day when she, too, would watch her Son being enthroned – but on a cross, John 19:25.

6. While Solomon was on the throne, kings from neighboring countries came to hear his wisdom and brought him gifts that included gold, silver and spices, 1 Kings 10:23–25. Similarly, sages from far away brought gifts of gold, frankincense and myrrh to the child Jesus, Matthew 2:11. Little might they

have known that they were presenting them to One whose wisdom was greater than that of Solomon, Matthew 12:42, 1 Corinthians 1:24.

2B

⚜ THE ROYAL ANOINTING ⚜

King George VI of England died while Princess Elizabeth was on tour in Africa with her husband, Prince Philip. She returned to England immediately for her father's funeral and was anointed into office as Queen. However, her coronation took place only some months later and was an event that involved considerable pomp and ceremony. Similarly, Jesus was anointed – through baptism – into office early in His ministry and His coronation took place some time later.

1. Though the Gospels stress the role of John the Baptist in preparing the way for the breaking in of the Messianic Age, we know little about where John operated. John, in his Gospel, states that the Baptist worked at Bethany beyond the Jordan (1:28), and at Aenon near Salim, 3:23. For many people in John's day, Jerusalem and the Temple were the focal point for all worship, thinking and living. However, John called the people into the wilderness – away from the world of pomp, power and things!

2. John directed a verbal barrage against those who prided themselves on their descent from Abraham, Matthew 3:9. He pointed them beyond their pedigree to a Person who would soon appear. He told them that the Messianic Age was about to break in. The people had hoped that it would be awaiting them in Judah after their return from Babylon in 538 B.C. (Isaiah 51:1–3), but it was not. But the time had now come for it to appear! However, the Messianic Age would not mean a life of prosperity, ease and leisure. Rather it called on everyone who had two coats to give one to a person who had none. Tax collectors were to be scrupulously honest in all their dealings. Soldiers were to be finished with extortion, and to be content with their pay. (See Luke 3:10–14.) This is still radical today!

3. Jesus of Nazareth presented Himself to John the Baptist for baptism (their mothers were related, Luke 1:36). While the baptism took place, some remarkable things happened.

   a) The heavens were torn open, and the Holy Spirit manifested His presence above Jesus' head in a manner that resembled a fluttering dove, Luke 3:21,22. The people had long hoped that God would rend the heavens asunder and come down to rescue them, Isaiah 64:1,2. It was now happening!

   b) While Jesus was being baptized, a heavenly voice declared, "You are my Son, the Beloved; with you I am well pleased," Luke 3:22. The first part of the statement is a quote from Psalm 2:7, a psalm used when a king from the line of David was enthroned. Its use at Jesus' baptism declared that Jesus was being anointed into office as King! The second part of the statement is the first verse of Isaiah's first Servant Song, Isaiah 42:1–4. Its use at Jesus' baptism declared that this King was to walk the way of a Servant! (See illustration 2C, top right.) The anointing into office has taken place. The coronation is still to come!

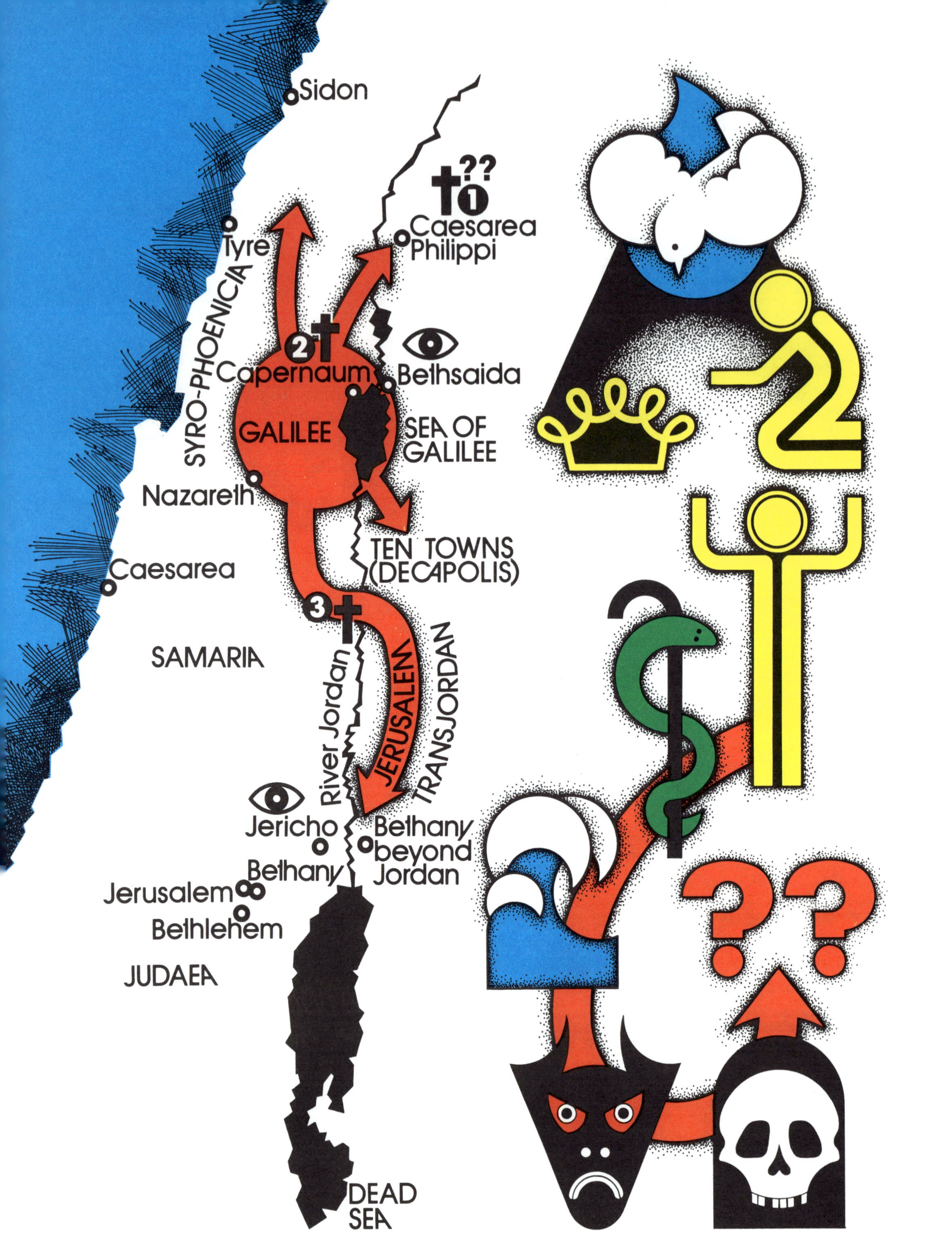
Sidon
??
1
Caesarea Philippi
Tyre
SYRO-PHOENICIA
2
Capernaum
Bethsaida
GALILEE
SEA OF GALILEE
Nazareth
TEN TOWNS (DECAPOLIS)
Caesarea
3
SAMARIA
River Jordan
JERUSALEM
TRANSJORDAN
Jericho
Bethany beyond Jordan
Bethany
Jerusalem
Bethlehem
JUDAEA
DEAD SEA

2C

⚜ The Royal Itinerary ⚜

How long did Jesus' ministry last, and where did His travels take Him? Some, on the basis of John's Gospel, suggest that Jesus' ministry lasted three years – pointing to the fact that John makes three references to Passover (2:13, 6:4, and 11:55). However, the first reference links Passover to the cleansing of the Temple – which the other three Gospels place during the last week of Jesus' ministry. The question might well be asked: Is John's primary concern with chronology, or with showing how Jesus reinterpreted and transformed Jewish beliefs and practices? On the other hand, Mark (whom Matthew follows closely, and whom Luke follows less closely) states that Jesus' travels were approximately as follows:

1. Accepting the location for John the Baptist's work as initially Bethany beyond the Jordan, Jesus' baptism and temptation took place somewhere just north of the Dead Sea, Mark 1:1–13.

2. The bulk of Jesus' ministry took place in Galilee itself, Mark 1:14–7:23. However, during this period He did cross the Sea of Galilee and minister on its eastern shore, Mark 5:1–20. Jesus also ministered in non-Jewish territory such as Phoenicia (Mark 7:24–30), and the Decapolis, 7:31–8:10.

3. After working in the Decapolis, Jesus headed north for Caesarea Philippi. Along the way, He healed a blind man in two stages at Bethsaida, Mark 8:22–26. After leaving Bethsaida, He began openly asking the disciples who the people at large, and who they themselves, thought He was, Mark 8:27–30. Peter, speaking on behalf of the disciples, said they had come to the conclusion that He was the Messiah (Mark 8:29); Jesus told them to say nothing to anyone about Him, Mark 8:30.

4. Jesus then predicted for the first time His coming passion in Jerusalem, Mark 8:31. The disciples responded with disbelief, Mark 8:32. A Messiah who would finish up on a cross did not appeal to them! Jesus rebuked the disciples for their attitude, and proceeded to explain what it meant to be involved with Him, Mark 8:34–38. (See also 9:30–32, 10:32–34.)

5. Jesus then headed south toward Jerusalem. He left Galilee (Mark 10:1), and entered Jerusalem, Mark 11:1. Along the way, He healed another blind man, Mark 10:46–52. He entered Jerusalem on Palm Sunday, and was crucified five days later.

6. Luke's scheme is a little different. After Jesus' baptism and temptation, He heads for Galilee and remains in Galilee. He does not minister in Phoenicia or the Decapolis. Furthermore, Peter's confession takes place in some unnamed place in Galilee, Luke 9:18–20. The reason for this is that Luke wrote *two* New Testament books. In his Gospel, he outlines Jesus' ministry to the *Jews.* In Acts, he outlines Jesus' ministry to the *Gentiles* through the apostles.

The evangelists share a common theme: Jerusalem is the city of opposition to Jesus, Mark 3:22, 7:1. He must finally go there to be put to death. His "coronation" must take place there! Let's follow Jesus on His long road to coronation.

2D

⚜ The First Sermon in the royal Hometown ⚜

A memory that often sticks in preachers' minds is that of delivering their first sermon in their hometown – when all the locals turn out to hear if they have anything worthwhile to say. Here is the story of Jesus' first "sermon."

1. Jesus grew up in Nazareth, and Nazareth had a synagogue. Significantly, Jesus did not make Nazareth the base for His ministry. He chose Capernaum, on the northwest corner of the Sea of Galilee. The ruler of Galilee, Herod Antipas, was as brutal as his father, Herod the Great. In making Capernaum His base, Jesus and His disciples could slip across the Jordan at the northern tip of the Sea of Galilee to enter the territory of Philip. Philip was also a son of Herod the Great, but by a different wife. He was much more moderate than Herod Antipas.

2. Jesus, while visiting Nazareth and worshiping in the local synagogue on a Sabbath day, was apparently invited to read from an Old Testament scroll and comment on the reading. He read the well-known Isaiah 61:1–6. But in reading the passage, He edited it!

   The passage extended hope to the Jews, with the prayer that God would wreak vengeance on the Gentiles, Isaiah 61:2 (second line). The passage stated that the day would come when the Gentiles would care for the Jews' flocks, till their land and care for their vines, 61:5. The Jews, freed of such tasks, would be able to devote themselves full-time to the worship of God as God's priests, 61:6a. The wealth and treasures of the nations would flow into the Holy Land so that the Jews might enjoy them and glory in them, 61:6b.

3. However, when Jesus read the passage, He left out all references to vengeance on the Gentiles, all references to the Gentiles serving the Jews, and all references to the wealth of the Gentiles flowing into the coffers of the Jews.

4. The audience initially accepted what Jesus had to say. When they began to understand the implications of His words, they turned on Him, Luke 4:20–24.

   Jesus did not withdraw what He said. He went further, pointing out that though there were many needy widows in Israel during the time of Elijah, the prophet was sent to minister to a *Gentile* woman in Zarephath in Phoenicia, Luke 4:25,26. And though there were many lepers in Israel during the time of Elisha, the prophet ministered to a *Gentile*, Naaman the Syrian, Luke 4:27,28.

   That was the last straw for Jesus' audience. They drove Jesus out of Nazareth, and considered throwing throw Him off a cliff to His death, Luke 4:29.

5. Remarkably, in Luke we never read of Jesus ministering in Nazareth again. Little wonder! But then, what took place in Nazareth was just a foretaste of things to come.

There are those who say that the Jewish authorities put Jesus to death because they did not understand Him. The truth is that they killed him precisely because *they did understand Him*!

Unit Two

Questions for Reflection

1. Read 2 Samuel 5:6–10a.

    a. How did Jerusalem come to be known as "the city of David" in the Old Testament narrative?

    b. What is the city of David in the New Testament, Luke 2:4?

    c. How do you explain the change?

2. Read 1 Kings 10:23–25. How might this passage relate to the visit of the Magi, Matthew 2? (Note also Matthew 12:42, 1 Corinthians 1:24.)

3. What does Isaiah 64:1,2 connect with the events mentioned in Luke 3:21,22?

4. The baptism of Jesus is described in Mark 1:9–11, Matthew 3:13–17, Luke 3:21,22. To understand its significance, it is essential to understand two Old Testament passages, Psalm 2:7 and Isaiah 42:1–4. Psalm 2, a coronation psalm, was used when crowning a king from the line of David. Isaiah 42:1–4 is the first of Isaiah's "servant songs." What traces of these passages do you find in the words spoken at Jesus' baptism, and what do they signify about the nature of His future ministry?

5. Only John 1:29 and 3:23 tell us where John the Baptist carried out his ministry. It is traditionally held that Jesus was baptized at Bethany beyond the Jordan, and tempted just west of there in the Judean wilderness, Mark 1:9–13. Where does Jesus travel in the following passages?

    a) Mark 1:14
    b) Mark 5:1,21
    c) Mark 7:24–30
    d) Mark 7:31, 8:10
    e) Mark 8:22,27
    f) Mark 10:1, 11:1

6. According to Mark (and Matthew 21:1 and Luke 19:29), Jesus entered Jerusalem for the first time during His ministry on Palm Sunday. Why might He have kept away from it?

7. Read Isaiah 61:1–7.

   a) In 61:2, the people pray for vengeance. On whom?

   b) According to 61:5, what role would the Gentiles play in the hoped-for postexilic messianic community?

   c) To what would the postexilic Jews devote their full attention, 61:6a?

   d) Whose wealth and riches would become theirs to enjoy, 61:6b?

8. Jesus used Isaiah 61:1–6 as the text for His first sermon in the synagogue of His hometown, Nazareth; see Luke 4:14–30.

   a. How did He reinterpret it?

   b. How did His hearers respond and why?

UNIT 3

⚜ ROYALTY IN ACTION ⚜

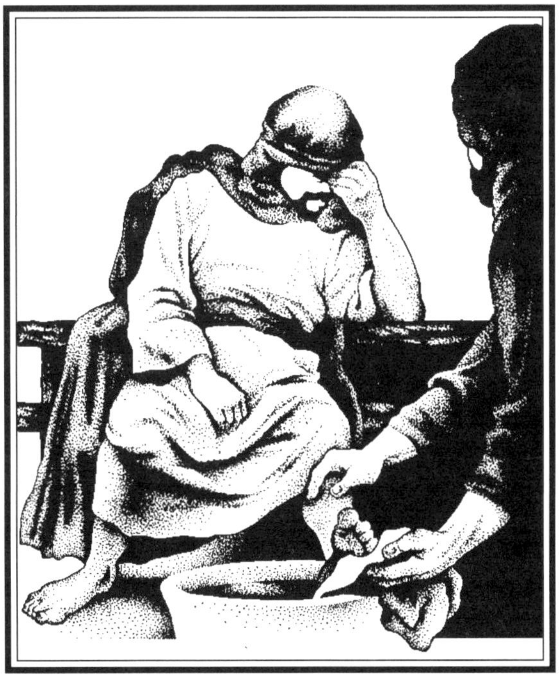

3A

⚜ The Royal Chapel ⚜

Visitors to Europe often tour the magnificent cathedrals that dot the landscape. The worship centers that dotted the landscape in Jesus' day were hardly works of art. They were synagogues that were basic in construction and functional in design. In addition to serving as a center for Sabbath worship, they served as the town school and meeting hall. Jesus did have at His disposal one remarkable building of magnificent design and proportion: Herod's Temple in Jerusalem.

1. In Jesus' day, a long-standing controversy raged: Where should God's people worship God? The Samaritans insisted on Mt. Gerizim. The Jews insisted on the Temple on Mt. Zion in Jerusalem. Naturally, the Jews despised the Samaritans. Sirach (apocryphal) 50:25,26 stated that God detested the Edomites and the Philistines – and the foolish people that live in Shechem: the Samaritans, who were not worth referring to as a people! The feeling was mutual: The Samaritans despised the Jews. Jesus, however, related kindly (though firmly) to the Samaritan woman at the well, and told her that the time was coming – indeed, had already come – when geography would no longer play a role in where people worship! With Jesus' coming, people can worship God in spirit and in truth, John chapter 4.

2. Joseph and Mary took Jesus to the Jerusalem Temple as an infant (Luke 2:22), and regularly in His growing years for the observance of Passover, Luke 2:41. Jesus Himself entered Herod's Temple for the first time *during His ministry* five days before His death, Mark 11:1, Matthew 21:1, Luke 19:45. When He entered it, He attacked those who controlled it, accusing them of funneling money out of other peoples' pockets into their own.

3. Jesus regularly participated in the life of the synagogue on Sabbath days. Yet He met people wherever they were, everyday: in their homes, on the seashore, in the towns and villages, on the surface of the Sea of Galilee, out in the countryside where He could point to life on farms, in orchards and among vineyards. Because creation was Jesus' cathedral and daily life His sermon theme, He could tell stories about everyday life that everyone understood, and point to birds, sheep and oxen that were a familiar sight. Remarkably, we never read of Jesus offering a traditional sacrifice during His ministry. However, He once did offer a sacrifice – Himself!

4. In Jesus' day, the religious leaders would have insisted that the "glory of God" dwelt in the Jerusalem Temple, specifically above the "foundation stone" in the center of the floor of the Holy of Holies. That location was considered to be the link between heaven and earth, the point in creation at which God met humanity, the navel of the earth from which creation grew, Genesis 28, John 1:51.

5. However, the glory of God shone around the shepherds the night of Jesus' birth, Luke 2:9. It manifested itself in and around the presence of Jesus at His transfiguration, Luke 9:32; see 9:28–36. It revealed itself at the crucifixion, John 17:1–4. It will reveal itself on that Last Day when the Lord of All summons humanity before Him, Matthew 25:31.

Sometimes today when the crowds are big, when the hall is huge and the preacher is waxing powerful, Jesus might be out in the back streets befriending the lonely, serving the needy, and talking to two or three who have never heard about Him before!

3B

⚜ The Royal Strategy ⚜

(See illustration 2C.)

During His ministry, Jesus might have walked around the countryside and through the streets of the towns and villages proclaiming: "Come, everyone! The Messianic Age has broken in! I am the Messiah! Come, gather around!" He did not do that. Why?

1. In Jesus' day, Palestine was a troubled land. After the Romans took control in 63 B.C., they tolerated no political opposition whatsoever. Thousands of zealots and ordinary people lost their lives in uprisings against them. During an uprising in A.D. 6, the Romans crucified 2,000 Jewish zealots.

2. The Romans were familiar with Jewish notions about a messianic deliverer. Had Jesus declared Himself to be such a person, the Romans would have interpreted the claim in political terms – and responded swiftly and brutally.

3. Jesus needed to get the message across to His followers that He was indeed the Messiah–even if He was not the kind of Messiah that the disciples and the people at large were expecting. He revealed His Messianic identity through His actions rather than through spoken words. Those who knew anything about Old Testament history and traditions should have been able to read the signs, which are described below. See also illustration 2C, lower *right.*

    a) *Serpent around a staff, a symbol of healing,* Numbers 21:9: Isaiah had written that when the Messianic Age broke in, the blind would see, the deaf would hear, the dumb would speak and the crippled would walk; see Isaiah 35:5,6. Jesus gave sight to the blind, hearing to the deaf, speech to the dumb and healthy bodies to the crippled; see Mark 8:22–26 and 10:46–52; Mark 7:31–37; Mark 2:1–12.

    b) *Storm-tossed waves*: The Jewish people never became a sea-faring people. They were, by and large, afraid of the oceans and storms at sea. They took comfort in the fact that God could control the oceans, the storms and the winds, Psalm 89:9, 107:23–32. Jesus stilled the storms (Mark 4:35–41), and walked on the waters, Mark 6:45–52; John 6:16–21.

    c) *Demonic face*: The Old Testament contains only a few references to Satan (e.g. 1 Chronicles 21:1). Jesus, as it were, flushes out the reality of the demonic, teaching that the demonic is every spirit, power, institution or pressure that sidetracks people from living to serve God and others into living to serve themselves.

    d) *Tombstone, symbolizing death*: A number of Old Testament passages stated that when the Messianic Age broke in, the dead would be raised, Isaiah 25:8, 26:19, Daniel 12:1–3. In raising the dead (Mark 5:21–24a, 35–43; Luke 7:11–17, John 11), Jesus declared that the Messianic Age had broken in!

After performing the signs in 3a, 3b and 3d (above), Jesus took the disciples north toward Caesarea Philippi. He asked them who the people at large, and they themselves, thought that He was, Mark 8:27–30. They replied that the people thought Him to be John the Baptist returned to life, Elijah or one of the prophets. But they themselves had come to a different conclusion!

3C

⚜ The Royal Confrontation ⚜

When Jesus asked about His identity, Peter answered on behalf of the group, "You are the Messiah!" (Mark 8:30). It seems the disciples had read the signs correctly.

1. Possibly the disciples expected Jesus to follow up with something like this:

    > I am glad that you recognize who I am. Well done! It is a joy to have you as my associates. Let's now go to Jerusalem, where we can expect the religious leaders and the people at large to come to the same conclusion. Before long they will all acclaim Me – and you! The future for all of us will be exciting!

2. Jesus did not say that. Mark writes (8:31):

    > Then he began to teach them that the Son of Man must undergo great suffering, and be rejected by the elders, the chief priests and the scribes, be killed, and after three days rise again.

3. The disciples must have been speechless. Peter could not handle the situation. He took Jesus aside and began to rebuke Him. It would be interesting to have a videotape of what transpired when the disciple confronted the Teacher!

4. Jesus retracted nothing. Rather, He told the disciples that those who wish to be involved with Him must deny themselves, take up their cross and follow Him. Those who wish to retain ownership and control of their own lives will lose them, while those who give life away by handing it to Jesus as Savior and Lord will find life. A person may, humanly speaking, gain control of the world – yet still own nothing and lose everything. (See Mark 8:24–38.) Though the disciples said nothing, they must have been shattered – and asked, "What on earth are we involved with?"

5. The cycle of (1) prediction, (2) confusion and (3) clarification took place again a few miles further south, just north of Capernaum, 9:30–35. Jesus predicted his passion. The disciples did not get the message. When the group entered a house in Capernaum and Jesus asked them what they had been talking about, they said nothing – they were ashamed to admit that they had been discussing who was, and would be, "Number One!" among them. Jesus told them that, in His kingdom, those who aspire to be "first" must strive to be "last" and the servant of everybody else! Another shock for the disciples!

6. It happened again – after Jesus and His motley royal entourage left Galilee (Mark 10:1) and were on their way to Jerusalem, Mark 10:32–45. There was a prediction (10:32–34), confusion (10:35–40), and clarification, 10:41–45. This time James and John asked to be shown a special favor: At Jesus' enthronement in Jerusalem, they wanted the honor of sitting immediately to His right and left in the coronation ceremony! Jesus informed the disciples that, in His Kingdom, things were different from the way they are in earthly kingdoms! In the world, greatness is measured in terms of how many people serve you; in His Kingdom greatness is measured in terms of how many people you serve. Without doubt, the disciples are now thinking, "This is not what we had in mind!"

⚜ The Royal Gift of Sight ⚜

The more we scrutinize the structure of each Gospel, the more we realize how carefully each has been put together, and how carefully we must study them. For example, immediately before Jesus' first passion prediction in Mark, He healed a blind man at Bethsaida, Mark 8:22–26. Immediately after His third passion prediction in Mark, He healed another blind man, Mark 10:46–52. In short, the three cycles of *prediction–confusion–clarification* are bracketed by healing miracles involving opening the eyes of the blind.

1. Initially, the first incident strikes readers as a little strange. People brought a blind man to Jesus and begged Him to touch the man. Jesus responded by taking the blind man by the hand and leading him out of the village. He then put saliva on his eyes, laid His hands on him and asked, "Can you see anything?" The man replied that he could, but things looked rather blurry. People, for example, looked like walking trees. Jesus touched the man's eyes a second time, and the man's sight was restored completely.

   We might well ask, "Why was it necessary for Jesus to touch the man a second time?" The answer becomes apparent only later in the Gospel.

2. The second incident appears less complex. As Jesus and the disciples left Jericho and headed for Jerusalem, they passed by a blind beggar, Bartimaeus, sitting by the roadside. Remarkably, though the man was blind, he called out, "Jesus, Son of David, have mercy on me!" Some of the onlookers told him to be quiet, but he repeated the cry. Jesus asked for the man to be brought to Him. The man begged Jesus to restore his sight – which Jesus did. The man in turn responded by following Jesus. His joy would have been a sight to behold!

3. Let's return to the first incident, in which Jesus touched the blind man twice in order to heal him. In a way, this blind man represented the disciples. They could "see" that Jesus was the Messiah, but they could not "see" what that would mean for Him – and for them. They needed a second touch. That second touch would come only after Jesus' resurrection.

   Bartimaeus, the blind man in the second incident, recognized Jesus despite his blindness; he could "see." His world was dark, yet there was light in his heart. His lips bore witness to that light. The disciples could see with their eyes, but they were blind in their hearts.

4. Mark's resurrection narrative (16:1–8) is brief. On the Sunday following Jesus' crucifixion, three women set out for Jesus' tomb to finish embalming His body, which had been buried in some haste. They expected to have to roll the stone away from the tomb. Instead they found the tomb open and empty. Yet it was not really empty! A heavenly messenger said to them:

   > Do not be alarmed; you are looking for Jesus of Nazareth, who was crucified. He has been raised; he is not here. Look, there is the place where they laid him. But go, tell his disciples and Peter that he is going ahead of you to Galilee; there you will *see* him, just as he told you.

   The word to note is *see*. The disciples were granted full spiritual sight only after the resurrection. Only then did they ask, in the spirit of Pilate's questions in John's trial narrative, "Just who is it that we are involved with? Where is He from? What has He done? What does it all mean?" Our answer must be that of Thomas, John 20:28.

Unit Three

Questions for Reflection

1. According to the Samaritans, the only legitimate place of worship was (and is!) on the top of Mt. Gerizim. According to the Jewish leaders at the time of Jesus, the only legitimate place for offering sacrifice was the Jerusalem Temple. What did Jesus do with both claims, John 4:16–26?

2. According to the Jewish religious leaders of Jesus' day, the "glory of God" dwelt in the Holy of Holies in the Jerusalem Temple. With the coming of Jesus, where did the glory of God manifest itself, Luke 2:9, 9:28–36; John 2:11, 17:1–4?

3. During His ministry, Jesus could not travel around proclaiming loudly that He was the Messiah. The Romans would have intervened quickly and brutally had He done so.

   a) What did Isaiah say would take place when the Messianic Age broke in, 35:5,6? How did Jesus fulfil these expectations?

   b) What did the prophets say would take place when the Messiah came, Isaiah 25:8, 26:19; Daniel 12:1–3? How did Jesus fulfil these expectations?

4. Compare Psalm 107:23–32 with Mark 4:35–41. What do we learn about Jesus' identity?

5. In Mark 8:27–30, Jesus asks the disciples who the people and they themselves believe He is. How do the disciples answer?

6. When Jesus finally defines the nature of His messiahship (Mark 8:31), how do the disciples respond (Mark 8:32), and what follow-up comments does Jesus make, Mark 8:33–38?

7. What takes place in Mark 8:22–26?

   What was the point of Jesus' action in touching the man's eyes a second time? (See Mark 16:7.)

8. In Mark's Gospel, Jesus predicts His approaching passion three times, 8:31, 9:30–32, 10:32–34. Two events involving giving sight to the blind bracket these, 8:22–26, 10:46–52. What message did these healing miracles speak to the disciples, and what question do they pose for us today?

THE MESSAGE OF THE ONE BORN TO BE KING

To plow through the respective accounts of the passion narrative in the four Gospels is a challenging task. However, when the digging is done and we become aware of the empty cross and the empty tomb, what is the "good news" that God wants each of us to hear? The story that follows describes vividly the biblical truth in relation to salvation:

In "I Married You," Walter Trobisch recounts an experience during a visit to Africa during which he gave a series of lectures on marriage and related matters. During this particular stay in Africa, Trobisch was driven around by a driver called Maurice. Maurice wanted to marry, but insisted that when he did, it would be to a virgin – a condition not easily met. Early one morning, during the close of his stay in Africa, Trobisch woke with a start and felt a strong inner compulsion to go to a bridge in the city. Maurice saw to it that he got to the bridge in a hurry. When the two arrived, they saw a woman standing in the middle of the bridge, looking down into the swiftly-flowing flooded stream below. She was deeply distressed, and preparing to commit suicide.

Trobisch knew the woman and her background. He had already been trying to help her. Her life had been one of moral and spiritual chaos. She was tormented by the memories of her many illicit love affairs and her numerous other gross sins. She felt she could not bear the burden of these memories any longer. However, Trobisch was able to persuade her not to kill herself, and eventually God used him, and others, to bring her to a joyous faith in Jesus as her Savior and Lord.

While Trobisch was talking to the woman on the bridge (her name was Fatma), Maurice remained in the car and prayed. While he prayed, something remarkable happened – of which Trobisch was to learn only later.

Eventually the day arrived when Trobisch and his wife Ingrid left Africa to fly back to Europe. A number of friends came to say farewell to them. Among them was Maurice – with Fatma standing next to him. As the Trobischs left the terminal to board the aircraft, Maurice pushed a letter into Trobisch's hand, asked him to read it only after take-off, and to send him a reply as soon as possible. After the plane reached cruising altitude, Trobisch read the following:

> Walter, when I prayed in the car on the bridge while you were talking to Fatma, a voice came to me as clear as a bell. It said, "This girl with whom Walter is talking will be your wife." It was crazy. I had never seen her before and had no idea who she was, or what she looked like. Could this have been God's voice? Please send me a telegram "Yes" or "No" from the next stop.

Trobisch shared the contents of the letter with his wife and commented, "Poor Maurice. He wanted so much to marry a virgin, and it looks as though he'll finish up with Fatma." Ingrid thought for a while and eventually responded, "But Walter, Fatma is a virgin now. She is washed in the blood of Jesus. She is without spot, without wrinkle, without blemish – as the bride of Christ. Maurice will marry a virgin!"

The Trobischs sent Maurice a prompt reply: "Yes!"

UNIT 4

⚜ ROYALTY IN THE HOLY CITY ⚜

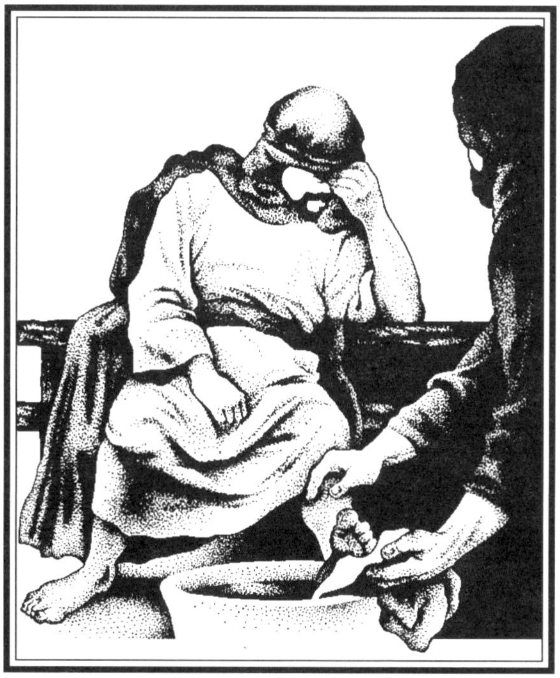

4A

⚜ The Royal Entry ⚜

Coronations are rare today, but some do occur. They are usually dazzling events. The new monarch travels in magnificent style in a royal coach from the royal residence to the cathedral where the event is to take place. The streets are lined with cheering people. The cathedral is crowded with national and international dignitaries. Those appointed to conduct the ceremony are ornately gowned and have prepared their rituals and speeches carefully. The royal attendants see that everything is in place and carry out their duties in a regal manner. No doubt as the monarch enters the cathedral, excitement runs high. Many people wonder, "What will the future bring?"

1. On that first Palm Sunday morning so long ago, emotions were high and questions were asked. The central figure, Jesus, had indeed come from a royal residence, the home of His Heavenly Father. But none present seemed to be aware of this.

2. The setting for the royal entry was spectacular. Standing on the Mount of Olives, Jesus could have seen the blue line of the Dead Sea and the hills of Moab to the east. But Jesus was no doubt looking west rather than east. Below Him lay the Kidron valley. Rising up from it were the slopes of Mt. Zion, which were topped with the huge walls of the platform for Herod's Temple. And there stood the Temple itself, glowing white in the morning sun with its gold ornamentation reflecting the sun's rays.

3. The royal vehicle was simple– a donkey. The only touches of luxury were the cloaks that the disciples threw across its back for Jesus to sit on.

4. The crowds were there too. They expressed their inner emotions with shouting, rejoicing and singing, yet they did not really understand what was taking place. The "royal attendants," the disciples, no doubt were experiencing an emotional high – but most likely they saw the future only in terms of the pomp and power it might bring to them.

5. Dignitaries were there, too – the religious leaders, the politically powerful, the rich, and perhaps others. Some would have been merely curious. Some would have been concerned – and already concocting plots to deal with Jesus, whom they perceived as a threat to their status and security.

6. Jesus, standing on the Mount of Olives and looking at the grand spectacle to the west, wept, Luke 19:41.

7. The royal entry began – not along a plush carpet or tiled cathedral floor, but along a windy, sandy and pebbly track.

8. The key events between the first and last moments of history were about to take place!

4B

⚜ The Royal Attack ⚜

1. Mark 11:11–19 tells us that after entering Jerusalem and looking around the Temple, Jesus left the city and went to Bethany – a mile or so to the east. Jesus cursed a fig tree the next morning (Monday) while returning to Jerusalem to attack the Temple, 11:12–14. When Jesus and the disciples passed by the tree on Tuesday morning, the tree was dead and withered, 11:20. At first, Jesus' actions appear a little strange, but their meaning becomes clear when we examine Micah 7:1–6 and Jeremiah 8:13. The rituals of the Temple were superficial and made little impact on the moral life of the nation and its people.

2. Both Matthew 21:12,13 and Luke 19:45,46 suggest that Jesus cleansed the Temple immediately after entering it on Palm Sunday. The issue is not chronology, but that in attacking the Temple, Jesus was signing His death warrant! Matthew also tells how Jesus cursed a fig tree on the day *after* He cleansed the Temple; in this case the tree withered at once, 21:18–20. Matthew alone refers to Jesus healing the blind and the lame after the cleansing episode, 21:14.

3. John places his account of Jesus' attack on the Temple at the beginning of his Gospel, 2:13–25. We should not presume that John is suggesting that Jesus' attack on the Temple occurred early in His ministry. The theme of *replacement* is key for John; it is likely that he is stating that Jesus replaced the Foundation Stone in the Holy of Holies as the presence of God on earth (1:51), and that Jesus and His followers are now the "Temple presence" of God among humanity, 2:13–15.

4. Jesus charged the religious leaders with using the Temple to enrich themselves, Mark 11:17b. In doing so, He reflected the spirit of Jeremiah 7:11.

   How had the religious leaders become so powerful – and, in some cases, so corrupt? It began, ironically, with the reform of King Josiah in 621 B.C., reported in 2 Kings 22:1–23:25. The Jerusalem Temple became the only place where Israelites could offer sacrifice to God. All other shrines were closed and destroyed, whether they were orthodox or pagan. Because people would find it difficult to lead or carry animals and other things to Jerusalem for sacrifice, they were permitted to sell their animals, etc. where they lived, take the money to Jerusalem, and buy again there. And because only designated coins bearing no image could be used in the purchase, moneychangers set up shop in the vicinity of the Temple. The ruling priests controlled these operations, which resulted in quests for power and money!

5. A directive in the Jewish Mishnah (commentary on the Law) forbade anyone to use the Temple platform frivolously – for example, to take a short cut when walking around Jerusalem. Jesus attacked people for doing that very thing, Mark 11:16.

6. Isaiah had expressed the hope that one day even the Gentiles would participate in the life of the Temple and its rituals; see Isaiah 56:6–8 and compare it to Mark 11:17a. In Jesus' day, any Gentile who dared go beyond the balustrade around the inner Temple was put to death!

7. Care must be taken not to tar all Jesus' Jewish contemporaries with the same brush. After all, Jesus was Jewish, as were His disciples and apostles, the first converts, and the members of the early church. The Christian church was established and initially built by Jews.

BALUSTRADE
To Bethany
Kedron Ravine
Gethsemane
Mount of Olives
GENTILES
WOMEN
MEN
PRIESTS

4C

⚜ The Royal Target ⚜

1. Herod's Temple was a massive and magnificent structure. When Jesus launched His attack on it, Herod's Temple was well on the way to completion. Its construction began in 19 B.C. It was finished in A.D. 63.

2. The southern Royal Porch was about 1,000 feet (300 meters) long and contained four rows of 40 columns, each 4.6 feet (1.5 meters) in diameter. The Sanhedrin (Jewish supreme council) met within its precincts. Solomon's Porch (eastern wall) was about 1,500 feet (457 meters) long.

3. The focal point of the Temple complex was the Holy of Holies in which, it was believed, the glory of God dwelt. The High Priest alone entered this part of the Temple, and only once each year – on the Day of Atonement. The stone in the center of the floor was supposedly the stone that Jacob used for a pillow one night at Bethel (Genesis 28) while fleeing from his brother Esau and traveling to Haran to find a wife for himself. That night, Jacob had a dream in which he saw a ladder reaching down from heaven, with angels ascending and descending on it, and heard God speak to him.

4. A balustrade (called the *soreq*) surrounded the Temple proper. It had thirteen entrances. However, only Jews were permitted to pass beyond the balustrade. A stone was set into the balustrade next to each entrance point; it bore this message:

   > Any persons who are not Jewish who pass beyond this point will have only themselves to blame for the death that will follow as a consequence.

5. The entire central structure was built on a platform about nine feet (3 meters) high. Then came, in ascending order and height, the Court of the Women, the Court of the Men, the Court of the Priests and the Temple itself.

6. Entrance to the Temple Platform was gained through a bridge (west wall), a huge staircase in the southwest corner (not shown), and the Huldah Gates in the south wall. The southeast corner of the platform was supported by a series of underground passageways and supports.

7. In Jesus' day, the Jewish leaders and teachers said that the Foundation Stone was the link between heaven and earth, the navel of the earth from which creation grew in the beginning, the place where Abraham was preparing to offer Isaac in sacrifice. It was also the place where the High Priest sprinkled the blood of a goat on the Day of Atonement. (Note carefully John 1:51.)

8. It is important to remember that Jesus did not attack the Temple itself. He attacked what was going on within it. Even so, to attack it in any way meant death! After all, 9,000 priests served on its staff and 80 percent of Jerusalem's population looked to the Temple for their source of income.

4D

⚜ The Royal Debating Style ⚜

Mark states that immediately after Jesus attacked the Temple, the Jewish religious leaders resolved to put Him to death, Mark 11:18. A series of confrontations between Jesus and the religious leaders followed.

1. *Mark 11:27–33*: When Jesus' opponents asked Him by what authority He was acting, Jesus responded by posing a question that hung them on the horns of a dilemma. Was John the Baptist and his mission of divine or human origin? Jesus' opponents recognized the trap and pulled out of the contest.

2. *Mark 12:1–12*: Jesus told a parable in which He pointed out that God had patiently looked for spiritual fruit among His tenants, those to whom He had entrusted the care of His vineyard (people) – but to no avail. God was now sending His Son in the hope of collecting what was due to Him. But that final ambassador would be put to death! This in turn would result in God taking control of His vineyard away from the present leadership, and giving it to others. Jesus' audience got the message and became all the more determined to do away with Him.

3. *Mark 12:13–17*: The Herodians were the next ones to take Jesus on. They asked Jesus a question designed to indict him no matter how he answered. The question had to do with paying taxes to the Romans. If Jesus had said, "Do not pay taxes to the Romans," they would have reported Him to the Romans and had Him charged with treason (even though they themselves objected to paying taxes to the Romans). If Jesus had said, "Pay taxes to the Romans," they would have objected, for they believed that they were under obligation to pay taxes only to God, who alone was their King! However, Jesus did not respond with an "either-or" answer, but with a "both-and" answer.

4. *Mark 12:28–34*: Next, a scribe approached Jesus in a more gentle spirit. He asked Him which commandment is the first of all? To understand the dialogue, one must bear in mind that the command to love God (the great *shema*) is in Deuteronomy 6:4,5, while the command to love neighbor is in Leviticus 19:18. Furthermore, the "neighbor" in Leviticus 19:18 is a fellow-Jew. There is reason to believe that, prior to Jesus, loving God and loving neighbor had not been joined. Jesus joined them – a radical move. Jesus said that those wishing to serve the invisible God are to serve that God full-time and without limit by serving other people full-time and without limit.

5. *Mark 12:35–37*: Jesus engaged in some verbal tussles with His hearers in which He pointed out that even David referred to his messianic descendant as his LORD (upper case, divine), not merely as lord (lower case, human). Jesus' hearers were looking into the face of their LORD, their God, but they refused to recognize Jesus for Who He really was.

We must remember that Jesus was not merely a meek and mild Person, who made every effort not to upset anyone. Still today, He sees only too well through the superficial and verbal games that people try to play with Him, and shreds them. His concern was, and is, to get beyond playing with words in order to proclaim His Lordship and to summon people into His Kingdom!

Unit Four

Questions for Reflection

1. Read Mark 11:1–11. In what way did Jesus fulfil, but also radically reinterpret, Zechariah 14:1–4a?

2. What "royal vehicle" did Jesus use when entering Jerusalem, Mark 11:1–7; note also Zechariah 9:9.

3. According to Mark 11:11–19, on what day did Jesus attack the religious leaders controlling the nation's religious life?

4. According to Matthew 21:12,13 and Luke 19:45,46, on what day did Jesus attack them?

5. John places Jesus' attack on the Temple at the beginning of his Gospel, 1:51, 2:13–22. In John, what was the "straw that broke the camel's back" for the Jewish religious leaders, 11:45–53? Note 11:1–44.

6. According to Mark, Jesus cursed a fig tree on His way to the Temple (11:12–14), and it was dead the next day, 11:20. Consider Micah 7:1–6 and Jeremiah 8:13 to determine the message of His actions.

7. How does Jesus handle His debating opponents in Mark 11:27–33 and 12:13–17?

8. What two commandments are given in Deuteronomy 6:4,5 and Leviticus 19:18? What did Jesus do with the "two" in Mark 12:28–34. See also Matthew 22:34–40.

Unit 5

⚜ The Royal Coronation ⚜ in Mark, Matthew and Luke

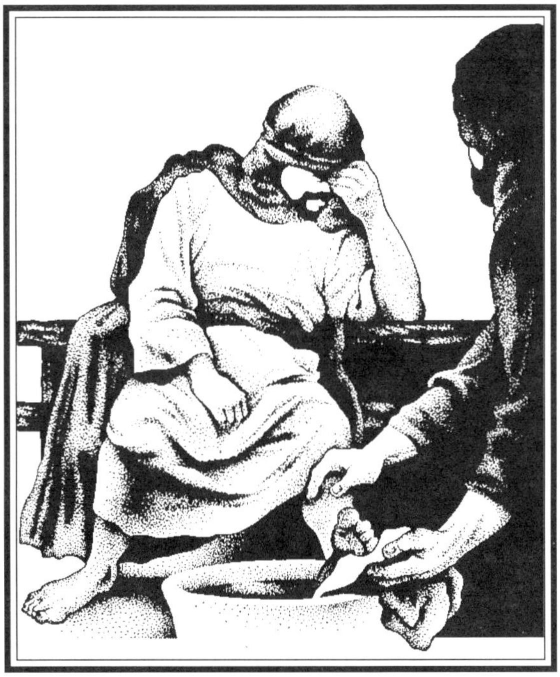

5A

⚜ The Pre-Coronation Banquet ⚜

In the royal homes of Europe, coiffed heads once dined in lavish style. No doubt banqueting went on in those rooms on the nights before and after a coronation.

1. On the night prior to His coronation, Jesus took the disciples to an upper room to share a meal with them. According to Matthew, Mark and Luke, the meal was a Passover meal; see Matthew 26:17–19; Mark 14:12; Luke 22:7. According to John 19:14, the Jewish *Passover* meal took place on the night that followed the crucifixion. (John had reasons for structuring his narrative as he did; see Unit 6.). All four Gospels describe Jesus sharing a meal with His disciples in an upper room during the evening prior to His crucifixion.

2. In Jesus' day, those who participated in a Passover meal recalled the events of the Exodus from Egypt. They also looked forward to the time when the Messiah would come to deliver them from foreign domination and usher in the Messianic Age.

3. Table fellowship anywhere is a relatively serious matter. This was, and still is, true in the Middle East where, to invite someone to share a meal is to bestow a great honor. To share table is to share life. It is an offer of peace, trust, brotherhood and forgiveness. When Jesus shared meals with publicans, sinners and His disciples, He expressed the message of His mission in action. He lived out the message of the redeeming love of God.

4. According to John, on the night prior to His crucifixion Jesus did more than share a meal with His disciples. He washed their feet, John 13:1–17. In Jesus' day, when a host welcomed a guest to his home, he kissed him on both cheeks and saw to it that his feet were washed and his head was anointed with perfumed oil. The Gospels do not refer to the disciples doing any of these things for Jesus. However, Jesus performed the task of a slave for them!

5. Jesus explains to them, "Do you know what I have done to you? You call me Teacher and Lord – and you are right, for that is what I am. So if I, your Lord and Teacher, have washed your feet, you also ought to wash one another's feet. For I have set you an example, that you also should do as I have done to you," 13:12–15. After Judas left the upper room, Jesus said to the disciples, "I give you a new commandment, that you love one another. Just as I have loved you, you also should love one another. By this everyone will know that you are my disciples, if you have love for one another," 13:34,35.

6. Those who know Jesus as Savior and Lord do not look to Old Testament commandments such as Exodus 20:4–17 and Deuteronomy 5:6–21 as their ultimate guide for life. These commandments were given to the ancient Israelites and contain details that applied specifically to them. After all, present-day Christians were not among those whom God "brought out of the land of Egypt, out of the house of bondage," Exodus 20:1–3.

7. The model for the godly is Jesus' life. This means that Christians are called to serve each other in all they do. The only way they can serve their ever-present but invisible Lord is by serving their ever-present but visible neighbor – who is everyone but themselves. In short, if everyone on Planet Earth asked, "How can I use life to glorify God by serving everyone else in community?", the world would be a very different place. It would be more as God intended it to be.

5B

⚜ Mark's Coronation Narrative ⚜

1. Mark's version of the passion history is given in chs. 14 and 15. Mark 14:1–11 outlines what transpired on the Wednesday of that final, climactic week; the remainder of these chapters describes the events of Good Friday. Why devote so much space to the events of one day? Jesus' life culminated very differently from traditional expectations. It was necessary to demonstrate that what appeared to be tragedy was really triumph.

2. On the Wednesday morning of Holy Week, the chief priests and scribes discussed how to get rid of Jesus, 14:1,2. That same morning, a woman anointed Jesus' head with ointment. The value of the ointment was approximately a year's wages, for a denarius was the usual amount paid for a day's work. Jesus accepted the gesture as a loving preparation for His coming burial, 14:8. Others expressed more mercenary concerns, 14:4,5.

3. Events followed in quick succession. Judas made arrangements with the chief priests for Jesus' capture. Mark does not mention Judas asking for money, though the religious leaders promised to give him some, 14:10,11. Preparations were then made for the celebration of the Passover. Jesus told His disciples they would have no trouble finding a room for the observance, for a man carrying a jar of water would lead them to it, 14:13. Usually only women carried water jars; men used water containers made of skins. During the Passover celebration, Jesus told the disciples that one of them would betray Him, but mentioned no name; see Matthew 26:14-16; Luke 22:3-6; Matthew 26:20-25; Luke 22:14,21-23; John 13:21-30.

4. The Passover observance utilized rituals and foods to remind the Jews of their miraculous deliverance from Egypt. It also pointed forward to the time when the Messiah would come to accomplish a second mighty deliverance for God's people. That night in the upper room, the disciples shared a table with the expected Deliverer. However, He had come to deliver them, not from the Romans, but from Satan, sin, death, judgment, damnation and themselves. With Jesus' coming, the Passover observance had completed its time of useful service. Jesus replaced it with another observance, one in which He gave to His new community His own body and blood together with the bread and wine that He passed around. During the Passover meal, Jesus told the disciples that they would all desert Him. Yes, even Peter would do that. However, after His death and resurrection they would meet Him again in Galilee, 14:28.

5. After the Passover observance, Jesus went with His disciples to the garden of Gethsemane. There, the realization of what was but a few hours away crushed Him. The disciples found it difficult to keep Him company in His prayer vigil and fell asleep. Eventually, Judas arrived with an armed group intent on taking Jesus into custody. Perhaps Judas' initial offer to the authorities was to lead them to Jesus at a time and place where there would be no opportunity for the crowds to protest. When greeting Jesus, Judas kissed Him; a kiss was the customary greeting that a disciple offered to his teacher. Jesus' capture frightened the disciples. They fled. Peter followed at a distance, but, when pressured, denied any connection with Jesus, 14:66-72.

6. Jesus' first trial took place at night, a factor that made the proceedings illegal. The members of the Sanhedrin (chief priests, elders and scribes) had assembled with the express purpose of doing away with Jesus as quickly as possible. However, the assembly had trouble with its witnesses. They were unable to agree about what Jesus had actually said. Finally, the High Priest confronted Jesus with a question, 14:61. He asked Jesus if He was indeed the Messiah, "the Son of the Blessed." ("The Blessed" is a Jewish term for God.) Jesus answered with, "I AM" (see Exodus 3:14), and continued with a statement based on Daniel 7 in which He declared that He was the "representative Israel" to whom the Kingdom of God had been given and in whom it existed. The High Priest responded by ritually tearing his clothes and accusing Jesus of blasphemy. His colleagues concurred, and demanded the death penalty. Jesus was then subjected to vile treatment, 14:53-65.

7. The next morning the Sanhedrin met as a body, no doubt to ratify the previous meeting's decision, and then sent Jesus to Pilate, the Roman governor. Though the Jews had judged Jesus to deserve the death penalty, they were not permitted to put anyone to death because they were a subject people. Only their Roman overlords could execute a criminal. The question Pilate discussed with Jesus is enlightening. He asked Him, "Are You the King of the Jews?", 15:2. Perhaps the Sanhedrin charged Jesus with claiming to be the king of the Jews to create in Pilate's mind the idea that Jesus was stirring up disloyalty to Rome. This charge was not valid, for Jesus' ministry was clearly non-political and posed no threat to the Roman authorities.

8. Pilate gave the people the opportunity to choose between Jesus and Barabbas. Barabbas had been involved in an insurrection and had killed in the process. In the minds of many Jews, his ambitions were more messianic than were those of Jesus. Pilate remained puzzled and perplexed. He had difficulty relating what the Jews said about Jesus to what he saw in Jesus. However, he handed Jesus over to his soldiers for scourging and crucifixion. Before they put Jesus to death, the soldiers sarcastically dressed Jesus as a king and paid Him mock homage. They then led Him out for crucifixion. Simon of Cyrene was pressed into service to carry Jesus' cross, 15:21. Before the soldiers fastened Jesus to the cross, they offered Him a drink designed to dull the senses and deaden the pain, but Jesus refused it, 15:23. They also divided His garments among themselves; garments were considered legitimate perquisites for executioners. Finally, at about 9 a.m., Jesus was crucified, 15:25.

9. When Jesus began His ministry, "the true Israel" numbered one person, Jesus Himself. As He carried out His ministry, the number grew to include Peter, Andrew, James, John, the other disciples and the crowds. As the thrust of Jesus' message became clear, the group diminished in size. The Jerusalem authorities, who had always been hostile toward Jesus, stirred up the crowds against Him. Judas betrayed Him. The disciples fell asleep in the Garden of Gethsemane and fled when His captors arrived. Peter denied Him. The crowds beneath the cross mocked Him. The thieves, who were his companions in death, reviled Him, 15:32. Furthermore, Mark reports only one word from the cross, "My God, My God, why have you forsaken Me?" 15:34. It seemed that even His Father had forsaken Him! Then came death. Jesus was so very alone.

10. Or was He? A Roman centurion stood beneath His cross and confessed the truth expressed in the opening verse of the Gospel ("the Son of God," 1:1), "Truly this man was God's Son!", 15:39. He confessed the very truth the Sanhedrin had denied. Joseph of Arimathea, a member of the Sanhedrin, assumed responsibility for Jesus' burial, 15:42-47. Some of the women who had been with Jesus took note of Joseph's activities.

5C

Matthew's Coronation Narrative

Matthew includes some unique details:

1. Judas asked the chief priests how much they would give him if he betrayed Jesus, 26:15.

2. Jesus named Judas as the one who would betray Him, 26:25.

3. Matthew makes no mention of Roman soldiers being among those who went to Gethsemane to capture Jesus, 26:47.

4. The whole Sanhedrin took part in the first trial at night, 26:59.

5. Judas repented of his actions, returned the money to the chief priests and elders, and hanged himself. The money he returned was used to buy a potter's field, 27:3-10.

6. Pilate's wife warned her husband not to have anything to do with Jesus; she was troubled by a dream, 27:19. Pilate washed his hands before the crowd, 27:24-26.

7. Like Mark, Matthew quotes only one Word from the cross, 27:46.

8. After Jesus' death (in which He yielded up His spirit, 27:50), the earth shook, rocks split, tombs were opened, and those who had been in those tombs appeared to many in Jerusalem *after Jesus' resurrection*, 27:51-53. These events reflect Ezekiel 37:1-14 and state that, in Jesus' passion and resurrection, the age of death is over and the age of resurrection has begun.

9. During the mockery scene in His passion, Jesus was given not only a crown, but also a mock scepter, 27:29.

10. The chief priests and Pharisees arranged to have Jesus' tomb sealed and guarded. The burial in Joseph's tomb, and the Pharisees' demand that Pilate post a guard, prepare the reader for the explosive events of the resurrection, 27:62-66.

11. Matthew's passion story contains a number of examples of how people reacted to Jesus in the moment of crisis:

    a) The Jewish leaders remained hostile, 27:39-44. The disciples deserted Jesus, 26:56. Judas gave in to despair, 27:3-10.

    b) On the other hand, the woman at Bethany anointed Jesus despite the protests of the disciples, 26:6-13. Pilate's wife pleaded on behalf of "that innocent man," 27:19. A centurion and his companions proclaimed Jesus to be "God's Son," 27:54. The women who stood beneath the cross attended to His burial, 27:56. The rich Joseph of Arimathea risked his reputation by burying a publicly executed man in his own new tomb, 27:57-61.

Most likely, Matthew intended his readers to place themselves into the story and to ask the question the disciples asked in the Upper Room, "Surely not I, Lord?" 26:22.

12. Throughout the events of the passion, Jesus remained the majestic Messiah of Israel. Though this theme is present in Mark, it is given particular emphasis in Matthew. Throughout, Jesus knew what awaited Him. He predicted what the Jewish leaders would do to Him, 26:12,18. He knew who would betray Him, 26:25. He predicted that Peter would deny Him, 26:34. His captors could not seize Him until He had confronted Judas with his treachery, 26:50. When the High Priest commanded Jesus to reveal His identity, Jesus predicted with majestic dignity His eventual exaltation to the right hand of God, 26:64. Those who filed past Jesus' cross jeered at Him and ridiculed His claim to be God's Son, 27:39-44. However, when death finally came, Jesus was acclaimed as the true Son of God and nature itself erupted to testify to Jesus' victory, 27:51-54.

5D

⚜ Luke's Coronation Narrative ⚜

Luke includes the following specific touches:

1. Satan entered Judas (22:3), who conferred with the chief priests and captains about how he might betray Jesus "in the absence of the multitude," 22:4,6. They agreed to give him money for his services, 22:5. Jesus did not permit Judas to kiss Him, 22:48.

2. The Jewish leaders themselves went out to capture Jesus, 22:52. Jesus healed the servant whose ear Peter had cut off (22:51) and was led away to the High Priest's house, 22:54.

3. No night trial or discussion is mentioned (22:54), but Jesus was subjected to abuse, 22:63–65. The Sanhedrin met in daylight and charged Jesus with claiming to be the Messiah, 22:66–71. (*Note*: The only body in Palestine that could determine whether or not a person was the Messiah was the Jerusalem Sanhedrin, which met in the Royal Porch of the Jerusalem Temple. Little wonder, then, that the disciples were keen to have Jesus go to Jerusalem. They were sure that the Sanhedrin would proclaim Jesus to be the Messiah and that they would benefit as a result!)

4. The authorities took Jesus to Pilate and leveled charges of political insurrection, 23:1–5. When Pilate heard that Jesus was from Galilee, he sent Him to his enemy, Herod, 23:6–12.

5. When Jesus appeared before Herod, the scene represented the climax of earlier accounts of Herod's reaction to Jesus, which shifted from fascination to opposition, 9:9; 13:31–33. Herod wanted to see a miracle, but all he saw was a silent prisoner who was the object of violent accusations and mockery. Ironically, the incident created peace between Herod and Pilate, 23:12.

6. Pilate felt convinced that Jesus was innocent and declared that he would chastise and release Him, 23:13–17. However, when the Jews demanded the release of Barabbas, Pilate yielded, 23:18–25.

7. Jesus spoke three words from the cross: "Father, forgive them; for they do not know what they are doing" (23:34); "Truly, I tell you, today you will be with me in Paradise," (23:43); "Father, into your hands I commit my spirit," 23:46.

8. Joseph, a member of the Sanhedrin, buried Jesus as an act of piety. He represented the righteous of Israel, who sought the kingdom of God, 23:50–53.

9. Some women prepared to anoint the body, but they were interrupted by the Sabbath. Jesus was buried, not like a criminal, but with honor, and His followers knew the place. When the women returned to the tomb to complete the anointing, there was no possibility that they had mistaken the place of burial, 23:55–24:3.

10. None of the Gospels suggests that the disciples or anyone else expected the events that were to follow the crucifixion. Even though Jesus pointed to His coming resurrection in the passion predictions (Mark 8:31; 9:30,31; 10:32–34), none of the disciples grasped what He was saying. When on one occasion they heard Him predict His resurrection, they were too afraid to ask what He meant by it, Mark 9:9,10. In all four Gospels, the resurrection explodes in on the lives of the disciples in a most unexpected manner.

Unit Five

Questions for Reflection

1. The Ten Commandments are given in Exodus 20:1–17 and Deuteronomy 5:6–21. What action of God was to move the Israelites to obey Him?

2. What is the pattern of life to which Jesus calls His followers, and what is to motivate them, John 13:12–15,34,35?

3. Read Mark's passion narrative in chapters 14,15. Read Matthew's passion narrative as outlined in 26:36–27:66. What details does Matthew provide in addition to those given in Mark?

4. Read Luke's passion narrative as outlined in 22:39–23:56. What details does he provide in addition to those given in Mark and Matthew?

UNIT 6

⚜ THE ROYAL CORONATION IN JOHN ⚜

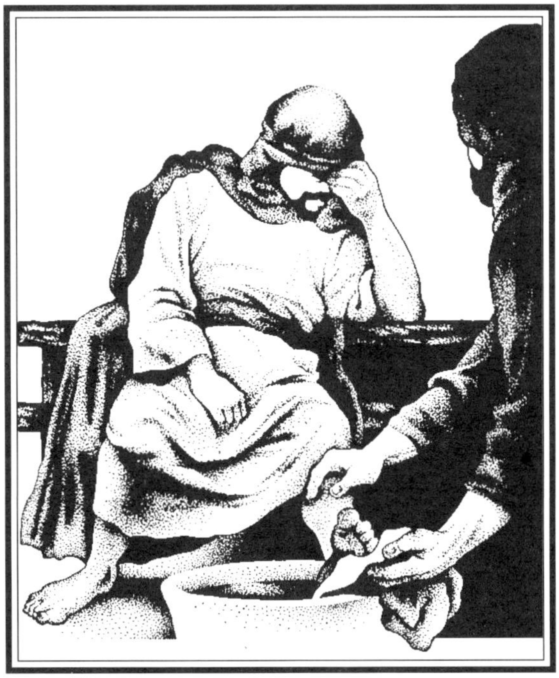

6A

⚜ JOHN: A ROYAL TRIAL NARRATIVE ⚜

1. When we study the four Gospels in depth, we sense the following:

    a) Mark reads like a "Manual for Discipleship."
    b) Matthew reads like a debate between Jesus and Judaism in a synagogue setting.
    c) Luke reads like an explanation of Jesus to the sophisticated Greek world.
    d) John's account is unique. It is said that the eagle is the only creature that can look directly into the sun. John soars and spirals at great heights like an eagle, close to the source of all divine light, and challenges us to look directly into the face of God. To sense the heights at which John's narrative soars, we must be aware of how he tells his story.

2. In Jesus' day, Jewish rabbis taught that the first thing God created was Genesis through Deuteronomy, the Pentateuch. They equated the Pentateuch with Wisdom, personified it, and taught that it was God's adviser in creation and the blueprint on which creation was based. More, Wisdom chose the Holy Land as its dwelling place and resided in the Temple, specifically in the Holy of Holies. John, however, equates the Word, the Creator and Wisdom with Jesus. In Jesus, the Word and the Wisdom of God became a Person; see John 1:1–14. More, though the Greek world said that the world of matter was evil and that only the invisible world of spirit was good and divine, John taught that, in Jesus, the Divine clothed itself in flesh, John 1:14a.

3. Though in Mark, Jesus exhorts the disciples to keep His identity a secret, John introduces Jesus' ministry by assigning to Him a series of titles: Lamb of God, 1:29,36; Messiah, 1:38; Teacher, 1:41; Son of God, King of Israel, 1:49; Son of Man, 1:51. To understand 1:51, see Daniel 7:13, and recall the role of the Foundation Stone in the Holy of Holies and the Day of Atonement.

4. Furthermore, there are hints that John has woven into his introductory section a reference to Genesis' seven days of creation. John 1:1 suggests *day one*. John 1:29 suggests *day two*. John 1:35 suggests *day three*. John 1:43 suggests *day four*. John 2:1 (four plus three) suggests *day seven*. Most likely, John presents Jesus as One who makes a new beginning to creation and history and brings the longed-for Messianic, eternal, Sabbath rest for God's people.

5. John then introduces a series of narratives in which Jesus replaces Jewish institutions, beliefs and practices with Himself and His Kingdom. For example, in John 2:1–11 Jesus creates a lot of wine at a wedding. The Old Testament depicts God's relationship with His people in terms of a marriage (Hosea chs. 1–3). Old Testament writers also said that when the Messianic Age broke in, God's people would sit under their own vines and fig trees (1 Kings 4:25; Micah 4:4) and that there would be an abundance of wine, Amos 9:13. John 1:48 sees this hope fulfilled in Jesus.

6. John's passion narrative in chs.18 and 19 contains very little about a Jewish trial. After Jesus' capture in the garden, He is taken to Annas who questions Him briefly about His disciples and His teachings. Jesus is then sent to Caiaphas, but we are told nothing about what transpired between Jesus and Caiaphas. Caiaphas merely sends Jesus off to Pilate. Note carefully 18:19–23; 18:24; 18:28.

7. As we shall see, John chs. 1–12 seemingly describe Jesus being tried by the religious leaders. Though in the first three Gospels, the straw that breaks the camel's back is Jesus' attack on the Temple, in John the straw is Jesus' action in raising Lazarus, John 11:47–53,57. Because the Jewish leaders have made up their minds about Jesus by the close of chapter 11, the Gentile world (represented by Pilate) must now make up its mind about Jesus.

6B

⚜ The Royal Trial ⚜ by the Jewish Leaders

1. In 2:1–11, Jesus turns an abundance of water (which would have been used for Jewish purification rites) into an abundance of wine – a symbol of the presence of the Messianic Age, Amos 9:13.

2. In 2:12–22, Jesus says that He replaces the Jerusalem Temple as the presence of God on earth. The authorities begin to question His authority to act as He does, 2:18.

3. In chapter 3, Jesus points out that membership in God's family is not dependent on physical descent from Abraham, but on divine rebirth. Genes do not count. Grace does!

4. In chapter 4, Jesus says that legitimacy of worship is not a matter of location, such as Mt. Gerizim or Jerusalem. What matters is worship in spirit and truth – Person, not place!

5. In chapter 5, Jesus slices through Jewish traditions regarding Sabbath observance. True worship is not demonstrated by an absence of activity but by the practice of compassion. His opponents are angry, and begin to persecute Jesus and plot His death, 5:16–18.

6. In chapter 6, Jesus repeats the wilderness feeding miracles, demonstrates His deity by walking on water, and says that He is the Bread of Life, the Messianic manna, come down from heaven (see 2 Baruch 29:8 in the Pseudepigrapha). Many of Jesus' followers desert Him at this point, 6:41,60,66.

7. In chapters 7 and 10, Jesus goes to Jerusalem for the observance of the Feast of Tabernacles and the Festival of Dedication (Hanukkah). The first of these celebrated the memory of the wilderness wanderings, the second the rededication of the Temple in 165 B.C. after the persecution of Antiochus IV Epiphanes of Syria. During these festivals, water was poured over the Temple altar to seek God's blessing on the coming harvest, and candles (symbolizing the Torah) were lit in the Temple courts. Though rabbis referred to their sacred writings as the Bread of Life, the Water of Life and the Light of the world, Jesus claimed those titles for Himself, 6:51; 4:7–15; 8:12, 9:5!

8. In John 9, Jesus healed a blind man on a Sabbath, causing the religious leaders to vent their wrath against Jesus and excommunicate the man from the synagogue, 9:22,34.

9. In John 10, Jesus speaks of Himself as the Good Shepherd. In Ezekiel 34, God said that He had had enough of Israel's "shepherds" (kings), and declared that He would now be their King and lead them back to an Eden-like land that they might enjoy the bliss of the Messianic Age; see also Ezekiel 36:33–36. In referring to Himself as the Good Shepherd, Jesus declared Himself to be that "Messianic God/King." The response was negative, to say the least, 10:19,20,31–33,39.

10. The Jews believed that when the Messiah came, He would stand on the Mount of Olives and raise the dead; see Zechariah 14 and Isaiah 26:19. Jesus' actions in raising Lazarus at Bethany on the Mount of Olives constituted a Messianic statement and gave rise to the final decision to put Him to death, 11:47–53,57.

11. Though the Jewish leaders acted throughout as though they were trying Jesus, the irony is that, in reality, Jesus was trying them!

6C

⚜ The Royal Trial ⚜ by the Gentile World

In the first twelve chapters of John, Jesus' words and actions relate directly to Jewish beliefs and practices. The Jewish leaders listen and observe, and John reports their reactions.

John's description of Pilate trying Jesus is carefully structured and comprises seven scenes.

1. *Scene 1* (18:28–32): The Jewish leaders bring Jesus to Pilate, state that they have already tried Him and sentenced Him to death, and ask Pilate to carry out the death sentence.

2. *Scene 2* (18:33–38): Pilate returns to his quarters, has Jesus brought to him, and begins questioning Him. Pilate's questions are pointed: "Are you the King of the Jews?" "What have you done?" "So you are a king?" When Jesus states that He is indeed a King, but the King of truth, Pilate walks away, and denies that it is possible to know ultimate truth.

3. *Scene 3* (18:38b–40): Pilate gives Jesus' accusers the opportunity to ask for the release of either Jesus or Barabbas (most likely, a zealot). They ask for the release of Barabbas!

4. *Scene 4* (19:1–3): Pilate orders his soldiers to flog Jesus, and they mockingly dress Jesus in "royal robes" as they do this. Though the soldiers' actions are designed to denigrate Jesus, the irony is that they express a divine truth about His Person. Jesus is indeed a King!

5. *Scene 5* (19:4–7): Pilate brings Jesus out to the crowds and twice says that he plans to release Him because he can find no case against Him, 19:4,6; see also 18:38. The Jewish leaders shout for Jesus' crucifixion and declare that, according to their Scriptures, Jesus must be put to death!

6. *Scene 6* (19:8–12): Pilate returns to his quarters, taking Jesus with him. Pilate is all too familiar with Roman beliefs about gods showing up in human form, and, with fear and trepidation, asks Jesus where He comes from. Jesus does not reply. Pilate reminds Jesus that he, Pilate, has the authority to determine whether Jesus will live or die. Jesus reminds Pilate that he can do nothing apart from what Jesus permits him to do. When Pilate again seeks to release Jesus, the crowd threatens to report him to Caesar and place his privileged status as a "Friend of the Emperor" in jeopardy. Note that territories controlled by Rome were classified as either "senatorial" (the governor was answerable to the Roman senate) or "imperial" (the governor was answerable to the emperor). Judah belonged to the latter category.

7. *Scene 7* (19:13–16): In the final scene, Jesus, Pilate and the crowds are together. Pilate presents Jesus to the crowds as their King. They respond by crying for Jesus' death. When Pilate asks "Why?" they (ironically) reply that their only loyalty is to the emperor. The charges they level against Jesus apply totally to themselves!

8. According to John 19:14, Friday is the Day of Preparation for Passover and Jesus is handed over at midday, 19:14. On this day at this hour, people who were gathered in Jerusalem began to bring their lambs to the Temple priests to be ritually slaughtered in preparation for the Passover observance. Jesus, twice called the Lamb of God (1:29,36), is handed over on the same day at the same time. He is the final, once-and-for-all Passover Lamb. Through the shedding of His blood, humanity's sin is dealt with once and for all.

9. Like Pilate, we must ask Jesus, "What have you done?" "What is truth?" "What kind of a king are You?" "Where are you from?" "What does all this mean for me?"

6D

⚜ The Royal Coronation ⚜

John 19:17–42

1. When Jesus walks from Pilate's quarters to Golgotha, He walks alone. No reference is made to weeping women or to Simon of Cyrene.

2. Jesus walks with dignity; no mention is made of Him collapsing under the weight of the crossbar. Jesus' hour has come! He is on His way to His coronation, and coronations are always dignified events! He is about to be "lifted up" on to His throne! He is about to show His Father's glory! (Here, note 17:1–5.)

3. Though Jesus is crucified between two men, no exchange of words takes place.

4. Pilate has an inscription nailed to the cross above Jesus' head. It reads, "Jesus of Nazareth, the King of the Jews." Though meant to be a bad joke, it expresses a sublime truth.

5. Solomon's mother sat on a throne to her son's right, 1 Kings 2:19. Jesus' mother stands on the ground beneath the cross on which her Son is being crucified. Jesus' first words from the cross have to do with the future care of His mother, 19:26,27.

6. When David fled from Absalom, Barzillai the Gileadite and two others saw to it that David lacked nothing, 2 Samuel 17:27–29. When David's descendant hangs on a cross, He cries out for something to drink, John 19:28.

7. Jesus' final words from the cross are, "It is finished," 19:30. He does not mean, "Thank God it's all over." Rather, He says, "I have completed the work I came to do." Jesus' executioners do not take His life from Him. Rather, He bows His head and gives up His spirit. He performs the ultimate act of the ultimate Servant: He gives up His life!

8. There is no need to break the bones in Jesus' legs to hasten His death. But then, the bones in Passover lambs were never broken; Jesus is the ultimate Passover Lamb, 19:31–33.

9. After a soldier thrusts a spear into Jesus' side, blood and water flow from the wound. The blood must be linked to the ritual of slaughtering the Passover Lamb. The water must be linked to Ezekiel's vision in 47:1–12. From Jesus, the true Messianic Temple, comes the healing stream that makes all things new.

10. Jesus' body is anointed with about one hundred pounds of myrrh and aloes, the traditional amount used in royal burials, 19:39,40.

11. Jesus' body is placed into a new tomb, 19:41,42. The body of a king was always placed into a new tomb.

12. Jesus' anointing into office as Servant-King took place when He was baptized, Mark 1:9–11. His coronation has now taken place. His people look beyond His throne to the empty tomb to hear the cry, "The King is risen! The Kingdom is established! The King lives forever!" And they ask, "My Lord and King, what would you have me believe? How would you have me live?"

Unit Six

Questions for Reflection

1. In Mark's Gospel, Jesus repeatedly tells the disciples to keep His identity a secret. However, John's approach is quite different. To illustrate, what is Jesus called in the following passages in John's Gospel?

   a) 1:29,36

   b) 1:38

   c) 1:41

   d) 1:49

   e) 1.51

2. Old Testament writers said that when the Messiah came, people would sit under their own vine and fig tree, and there would be an abundance of wine, 1 Kings 4:25, Isaiah 36:16, Amos 9:13. What, then, was the significance of Jesus' action at the wedding in Cana in creating a large quantity of wine, John 2:1–11?

3. The first twelve chapters of John constitute a trial narrative. Throughout it appears that the Jewish religious leaders are trying Jesus, when in reality Jesus is trying them. We have already seen the following: In John 2:1–11, Jesus replaces Jewish purification rites. In John 2:12–22, Jesus replaces the Jerusalem Temple as the presence of God on earth. In John 4, Jesus rejects the claims of both Jews and Samaritans concerning their respective "holy mountains." What practices, beliefs and institutions of Judaism does Jesus replace in John 3, John 5 and John 6? (In relation to John 6, note that the rabbis taught that when the Messiah came, the manna would fall from the sky again; see Joshua 5:10–12, 2 Baruch 29:8.)

4. The Jewish leaders referred to their scriptures as the Water of Life, the Bread of Life, and the Light of the World. What claims does Jesus make in John 4:7–15; 6:29–35; 8:12 and 9:5?

5. By the end of ch. 11, the Jewish leaders have determined that Jesus is guilty and that He must be put to death. Because this "false Israel" has rejected Him, Jesus must create a "true Israel"– and does so in chs. 13–17. Jesus' final trial is conducted by Pilate, the representative of the Gentile world. It takes place in seven scenes: 18:28–32; 18:33–38a; 18:38b–40; 19:1–3; 19:4–7; 19:8–12; 19:13–16. What takes place in each scene?

6. In Mark, Jesus is handed over for crucifixion at 9 a.m. on Passover Day, Mark 15:25. In John, Jesus is handed over for crucifixion at midday on the day of Preparation for Passover, 19:14. How do you account for the differences?

7. John describes Jesus' walk to Calvary as a quiet, dignified affair. Why? (In determining your answer, note that according to John 19:30, Jesus' life was not taken from Him – He gave it away!)

8. Though it appeared that Pilate was trying Jesus, in reality Jesus was trying Pilate. By extension, with what questions does Jesus confront each of us at every step along the way?